IOLAIRE

IOLAIRE
KAREN CLAVELLE

*Ali,
Hope keeps the
heart
Karen*

TURNSTONE PRESS

Iolaire
copyright © Karen Clavelle 2017

Turnstone Press
Artspace Building
206-100 Arthur Street
Winnipeg, MB
R3B 1H3 Canada
www.TurnstonePress.com

All rights reserved. No part of this book may be reproduced or transmitted in any form or by any means—graphic, electronic or mechanical—without the prior written permission of the publisher. Any request to photocopy any part of this book shall be directed in writing to Access Copyright, Toronto.

Turnstone Press gratefully acknowledges the assistance of the Canada Council for the Arts, the Manitoba Arts Council, the Government of Canada through the Canada Book Fund, and the Province of Manitoba through the Book Publishing Tax Credit and the Book Publisher Marketing Assistance Program.

Printed and bound in Canada by Webcom for Turnstone Press.

Cover image: Rod Read, *The Beasts of Holm*

Library and Archives Canada Cataloguing in Publication

Clavelle, Karen, 1948-, author
    Iolaire / Karen Clavelle.

Poems.
Issued in print and electronic formats.
ISBN 978-0-88801-611-9 (softcover).--ISBN 978-0-88801-612-6 (EPUB).--ISBN 978-0-88801-613-3 (Kindle).--ISBN 978-0-88801-614-0 (PDF)

    I. Title.

PS8555.L3917I55 2017   C811'.54   C2016-908181-8
                                                     C2016-908182-6

the *Iolaire* carried only seamen home, and over 200 of them she took.
She run into the Beasts of Holm.
She spilled them all into the sea.

FOREWORD

The letters in this long poem are fictitious constructs of the imagined character, Is, whose story derives from research on the *Iolaire* Disaster of 1 January 1919. They create narratives of personal loss and hope alongside, or within, the communal losses that are part of the *Iolaire* story, but they also look to some of the history of the villages in Scotland's Outer Hebrides to provide a backdrop against which more documentary accounts of the *Iolaire* Disaster press.

~

A word on names. The nicknames and foreshortened names that create confusion when family names are shared inter-generationally. The diminutive 'Is'—short for the Gaelic *Iseabail*, and the English Isabella—serves to affirm the character's being in a way, asserting: 'I think,' and 'I am.' Isabella is, and, insistent on being, she carries on as best she can, her plans for a life in Canada doubly disrupted by the Great War and the sinking of the *Iolaire*.

Is and DB marry while he is home on one-week leave, just before the Armistice of 1918. The letters begin with his leaving the Island for the last time. As the anniversary of the sinking of the *Iolaire* approaches, along with Is's acceptance of DB's death, the letters simply stop. '*Tha mi sgìth 's mi leam fhìn*,' Is writes to her friend, Morag, in early recognition of her loss, and later to DB, in resignation, 'I am tired and I am alone.' '*Tha mo chridhe-sa briste brùite*,' 'my heart is broken and bruised.' '*Gur mise tha fo ghruaimean*,' 'I am in despair,' she writes to DB, quoting more lines from a traditional Gaelic song expressive of loss, but not of completion.

That there is no closure to the letters reflects the fact that there *has been* no particular end to grieving on the Long Island, even as the 100th anniversary of the sinking of the *Iolaire* arrives. The story is still being told in poetry and song, prose fiction, non-fiction, and documentary. Among more recent accounts of the disaster are the BBC production, *Iolaire*, narrated by the late Nan S. MacLeod (2008); John MacLeod's

When I Heard the Bell (2009); and Malcolm MacDonald's book [title TBA, publication pending, Stornoway: Acair Press, 2018].

The grandchildren of those Lewis and Harris seamen lost to the sea have worked assiduously to reclaim their ancestral pasts. Many have written and collected volumes of material related to the *Iolaire* Disaster; one dedicated grandson holds 181 death certificates. With steadfast perseverance, he has collated a list of birth dates for all but two and death dates for all but eight of the seventy-four Island survivors of the wreck, five of them buried as far afield as Canada, four in Australia, and one in New Zealand. Fully one-third of the Island men lost in the *Iolaire* Disaster were never recovered from the sea, among them the imagined Murdo Domhnall (DB) MacLeod—Is's DB.

~

The letter from Is to DB dated 2 November 1918, addressed and stamped but never posted, was found in the same drawer as all the other letters, this one caught at the back of the dresser. The other letters had been bundled together with an RN Distinguished Service Medal in an embroidered silk hankie fastened with a faded and frayed red ribbon, each letter in an envelope, each addressed in Isabella's elegant hand, bearing only DB's name *in English*—Murdo Donald Macleod, RNR.

Some of the letters, handwritten in pencil, are water-stained and illegible despite Isabella's careful script. Some still contain Is's reference to local newspaper articles concerning the sinking of the *Iolaire* and the Royal Navy and Public Inquiries into the Disaster. Isabella's letters provide accounts of what was happening in her village roughly from the Armistice through to the first anniversary of the sinking of the *Iolaire* that effectively dashed any hopes the people of the Long Island might have had for a better life in the aftermath of the Great War. Although Isabella's letters recognize that life goes on, the poignancy of the Gaelic expression *Dh'iarr am muir a thadhal*, the sea asked to be visited, cannot easily be escaped.

HOME. They had survived the Great War and its peripheral hazards. And then they died, neither on foreign soil nor in foreign waters, neither by the enemy's hand nor of causes related to war. Because they would not be considered war casualties, their families would not receive the nominal benefits awarded to dependents and survivors of those killed in active service. Even the ritual delivery of the black-edged telegram and the kindly ministrations of the three bearers of bad news were denied them. There was nothing to mitigate the disaster that hit every family on the Island.

The Ratings came home and died there, in the harbour. They died in the very minutes that their families were waiting to greet them in the same harbour. They died in the minutes families were finishing homecoming preparations in the villages spread over the 45-mile length and 30-mile breadth of the Long Island. They died before they could embrace those who, like them, endured a long and distant absence from home. They died when they seemed most safe.

ABSIT OMEN

GOD WILLING ; GOD FORBID

Late afternoon and early evening Old Year's Eve, 31 December 1918. Hundreds of Royal Navy Ratings at the railhead at Kyle of Lochalsh wait to be ferried home to the Western Isles of Lewis and Harris— many of them for the first time in 4½ years. The air is electric. The Armistice behind them, they are scant hours away from reunions with sweethearts, family, and friends.

Iolaire wrecks barely yards from land, past Arnish Point and Tiumpan Head, at the Beasts of Holm, in the first hours of the New Year. 205 seamen drown. 82 survive. The youngest lost, 17, the signal boy from Aberdeen. The oldest, at 51, a seaman still.

31 Dec. 1918 *The Scotsman*

    Scotland—N Scotland, E Scotland. W and England SE
Light winds from between 7 and 8: freshening*
later: cloudy to dull: some rain, hail, or snow: cold,
becoming milder

* Wind velocity Beaufort 6: Fresh Breeze: 19-24 mph / 17-21 knots;
sea state: moderate waves 6-9 ft. taking longer
form, many white caps, some spray (Beaufort Scale)

past the point   past Arnish Point
         & Tiumpan Head
         & Holm Point
    they   were

curled fleece on the bow, wine to water
for *Iolanthe, Mione, Amalthaea*   Dom Pérignon

but for *Iolaire* strange fruit : *1919 cellars empty*
    vineyards profaned by ordnance,
    by no man's land corpses, arsenic, chlorine
    by 10-pounders and torpedo tubes of Hellespont

past the 37 million already-dead, but not
    past the taking   205 more

                   20 yards from *home*

Isle of Lewis, 2 November 1918

> 'Tha mi sgìth 's mi leam fhìn,
> Buain na ranaich, buain na ranaich
> Tha mi sgìth 's mi leam fhìn,
> Buain na ranaich daonnan.'

You're just away, but how much longer? I am tired. And I am alone. And I have been cutting the bracken. When will you sing for me?

There's talk of letting the fishing boats go now the war's over—all but over, God willing. The old Depot ship's gone, and a new Iolaire already in her place. Maybe they'll send everyone home. Imagine—the war over, the New Year coming, and in the spring, God willing. Oh, Murdo Domhnall DB MacLeod, DB, we'll be on our way to Ma-ni-to-ba.

There was a letter from Mary this morning. She says they've had snow at the farm since early September, frost since August. She doesn't mind the snow, but she misses her warm blackhouse and, oh, she says, for the smell of peat fires at home and the sound of the sea. She has had the Morisons with her since their house burnt down at the end of September—and Mrs. M's baby coming any day. So, hadn't they just nicely settled in when Mary's new family went from six to seven, and Mary makes eight. Five children, Mary says, and she didn't have to do a thing.

Two weeks married today—a fortnight, and it feels as though you've been gone two years and then some. It's odd being a newly married woman without a husband; odd for you too, I'd guess. I think how things would be if—if there were no war. If you had stayed in the Prairies, and I there with you. If you were here and I weren't knitting, no end to knitting, or writing letters—we would be off to bed, wouldn't we just?

One mitten a night since you left, that's all I can do. I can hardly see with just the one light. Oh, nam faicinn thu a' tighinn, if I saw you coming…

The wind blows cold in November.
love, Your Is

Mo Shràidh,

　Here, my Darling, is yet another letter you cannot read. (Censor, sharpen your pencil.) We have been several days ██████████████████████████████ ██████████████████████████████ We will ██████████████████████████████ ████████, ███████, █████████ I don't know. ████████, without question. My job is to ██████████ so my training at ██████████ will at last be put to good use. We've been ordered to ██████████ and will ███████ at █████. Here are your ███████████, as promised, from █████████. I've made worse trades than peeling potatoes for something I want! A week of KP! Cost me my fags too. You will smile the more, I hope, at my pleasure of first seeing you in them, then (something for you and the censors) my greater pleasure at helping you out of them. The ███████████ of the sea here in the ██████████████ is just like home when the sun shines, and the moonlight takes me home where we shall be together very long, soon.

　　　　　　　　　　　　　　　Always, DB

night watch

eight times to strike out the Old Year
eight more to strike the New
no more on the watch in the *silent* hours
when *the tide as moving seemed asleep*

. . . .

till the scrape of metal belly
the gneiss of the Beasts, till
Iolaire settles askew, gouged and broken,
in the chill light of the new day

SOMEONE should have taken responsibility: Commander Mason, as captain, or Rear Admiral Boyle, as Mason was under his command, or Boyle's superiors, including the First Lord of the Admiralty. Someone made arrangements for special trains. They were to transit hundreds of men from the South coasts of England north to Inverness and then south again to the railhead at Kyle. Too many men for the *Sheila* that usually makes the 70-mile trip from Kyle to Lewis, HMY *Iolaire* had been pressed into service to help transfer them home. Someone stopped short of seeing them home. Someone set everything in motion.

The mail steamer, the *Sheila*, had a scheduled crossing on Old Year's Night, but civilians and Ratings had been waiting on her since their arrival at Kyle the previous day. The *Sheila* had room for only 60 more. Hundreds arrived. The Movement Officers at Kyle marched 60 of the newly arrived Ratings on board. The officers marched the rest of the Ratings in single file onto the *Iolaire*. They settled in the chartroom, on the upper deck, below deck, in the lounge, in whatever space they could find on the crowded yacht. Harrismen snuck on to the *Iolaire* in the hope of getting home earlier, other men snuck off. The unhappy alternative to the *Iolaire*, although the Ratings seem to have had little choice, would have been to wait out the *Sheila*'s first trip back three days into the New Year.

At the inquiry, it was said Captain Mason felt additional passengers on the *Iolaire* would not be a problem. So, on a blustery New Year's Eve, the *Iolaire* set sail with a half-crew of 24, not one of them experienced in bringing the steam yacht into the narrow harbour. There were life vests for 80, lifeboats for 100, and 284 men on board.

...---...

HMY IOLAIRE
AGROUND and SINKING
300 on board
ABANDONING SHIP
40 minutes left

...---... ...---...

the dynamo was broken

. . . .

When none of the signals are available, attract attention by anything out of the ordinary. Flash with a torch. Knot any flag into a wheft and fly it upside down as a signal.

. . . .

the dynamo was broken

On his last morning in the village, I would have DB and Is walk hand-in-hand down the road to the sea. We would see them stop to sit in the marram grass, heads together, and dream their new life. 'I'll have my kist packed when you get back,' she would tell DB. 'Save a bit of room for your Paris shawl, Issy,' DB would say. He would look far out to sea and fall silent, and she beside him, and she would turn her new wedding band round and round on her finger, her chin trembling, her eyes threatening tears burning.

'Is,' he would say, 'you'll remember to soak the handle on the *tairsgeir* before you use it, will you?' And, 'Mother, she'll—. And the cat will keep the bed warm while I'm gone this last time, when she's not in her hammock.'

'Have you got your new socks in your kit?' Is would ask. 'And a good pencil?' And we would sense the silence broken when DB would tug her by the hand down the dunes to caves for shelter from the rising wind. And after they'd set their boots by the fire to warm, they would pick up the dream, and when it was time for him to go, I would have them part hoping for the future, leaving the Island for their life together.

The dreams are not new: just changed. The marram grass serves as a shelter on the sheep's paths close to the sand-cliff's edge. That I can neither see over it nor through it causes no alarm. The sky remains constant, and ever-changing too, as it is over the sea, but into the dreams inflected by place has entered the fleeting sense of a man I could not at first identify—like the sense of a lover in the moments before you slip back into longing. The perception brings such intense feelings of well-being that I try to hold myself in semi-sleep. When I open my eyes, I am pained with loss. The man is gone. The dreams linger, sensual as the burn of tweed on my cheek, the warm comfort in the arms of a hand-knit jersey, my fingers caught in thick freshly washed hair, a soft word, a beard, a deep voice. These memories belong to Is, too, grief-swamped and drowning. And in these mornings, when I mourn her loss, I wonder about my own.

from the cliffs nearby

greylag and barnacle geese grazing on the islands,
fulmars, and black guillemots,
razorbills, and kittiwakes, and glaucous gulls—
these, and waders took flight—
and, as the day dawned the local buzzards and gyrfalcons
left off patrolling the cliff tops for a closer look

FEARED HEAVY LOSS OF LIFE

Under the Command of Captain Richard Mason, HMY Iolaire set sail from Kyle of Lochalsh, about an hour before the mailboat on her last run of the Old Year. There was a freshening, fair wind from the south and Iolaire had an uneventful passage across the Minch. Little more than an hour into the New Year, she passed the lights at Arnish Point. Strife and hostilities behind them, spirits in coming home, anticipating New Year's reunions, on the very cusp of life beginning again, they ran aground on the Beasts of Holm.

2 January 1919

' 'S bochd an naidheachd 's gur brònach'

Dearest Morag,

All I can think is the proverb, 'Sorrow and ill weather come uncalled.' I am afraid I shall come undone with fear should I but let words out. What I write is me, but it is not me.

Do you mind the clipping I sent you on the MacPhail lad in Algeria—a couple of days at sea, and before that the only survivor from his ship? He's drowned at Holm. One lad had an engagement ring in his pocket; another two never apart in four years of war—one gone; one lad safe on shore gone back into the sea to find his brother; one lad home here, and nary a word out of him since; a lad's kit washed up at his home at Sandwick; lads washed up against the cemetery wall …

27 Nov. 1919

Mo Bhr`aidh,

   Petty Officer, to you now.
Went to Thanksgiving Service
for Armistice Day. People near
mad with excitement. I am
nearly mad for you. Aweigh
tomorrow back 24th. Get my
boots out. I'll be home at the
New Year. Start packing. DB

Mrs. DB MacLeod
11 .
Isle
Outer

...---... ...---... ...---...

the wireless was out

no answer

A G I must abandon the vessel

A Q boat is lost

B O I have lost all my boats

B S met with an accident

B Z am grounded

C A am grounded likely to break up
   require immediate assistance

C E I am aground; send what assistance you can

C H vessel on the rocks
   in distress; want immediate assistance

C L I am disabled communicate with me

C O can you assist

C Y render all assistance possible

...---... ...---... ...---... ...---...

D B send immediate assistance

D E will you assist me? (or vessel indicated)

E S boat in distress

F H send a boat

H M vessel seriously damaged

N A aground want immediate assistance
   am aground; likely to break up
      require immediate assistance
      boat in distress

N B cannot save the ship

N I have lost all boats

N O I am sinking

    send all available boats to save passengers and crew

N Q I must abandon vessel

N R I require assistance

    please remain by me

She sunk. Sunk with her head to the west, the men coming across on the rope, and when she went down, the sea washed some of them off, and some she washed ashore.

There was rockets: red, and white, and green sent up, and sirens were blowing and the sea was coming on board, and then she come off the rock and she come broadside onto the shore, you see, and there she was, her stern in and her head canted out, and the sound of the sea on the portside, striking heavy—no boat could live.

From the time she struck, maybe forty-five minutes, maybe an hour.

Some of them lowered the boats on the starboard side, and in the backwash they smashed against the ship's side, the weather side. There was maybe eleven or twelve men in my boat and three got back on board, and the rest, they got thrown into the sea. Someone pointed to a rope that was stretched from the ship to a small boat, and I said to him, 'You go first,' and he did, and I followed. And that's what I remember.

… and in the Gazette today: 'The villages of Lewis are like places of the dead.'

From the cliffs, you can see the fishing boats past the mouth of the harbour, trawling back and forth with their hooks and nets, and in they come, grim fishers of men.

Phemie and I went down to Sandwick for the first time today. Something small and dark was rolling in the waves, in and out it went, what's that, what's that. And then stayed a sailor's hat come right to my feet. And then I think, I just—well, I don't know. All I can think is the waves. And the sand going away under me, pushing and pulling, all wet, and sticking, and the stones rattling. Water burning cold through me. And never a word the two of us—both seeing the name, and then there was a boy come and Phemie sent him away to fetch Donald, and he took us away home in the gig.

Some of the lads was sleepin', but the water's a bit rough, an'…
I was just thinkin' to get home and then we come onto the skerries.

an' the lights went out, an' the tide was pullin' hard an' the wind's lashin' the foam up an' over the decks, an' the water's washin' us off.

I come up through the whins. You couldn't see nothin', just hear what was goin' on below, and bang. Like an aerial bombardment, maybe two. Might have been her boilers.

I come to in sick bay. Don't remember anything 'cept my sister standin' over me cryin', hollerin' for someone to come…

SERMON

We offer today prayers of thanksgiving for the miracle of survival for men from the floundered *Iolaire*, for the men whose lives have been spared. And we offer prayers of intercession, prayers that God will comfort us in our terrible grief for those lost.

We ask who should take credit. Who should take responsibility and blame? God deserves some of the credit for the rescue and survival, but if we say God heard the prayers sent for these survivors, what do we say of the prayers of the lost? Who was watching when *Iolaire*'s path grounded her on the Beasts? Could not God have changed her path? Were some men somehow more deserving of God's care than others? Some families more deserving than others? Some wives more deserving of husbands? Some children of fathers? There is no escaping these questions, and what answers there are will not always satisfy us.

Where *was* God? The Bible gives us stories of the presence of God when in need we might ask it, and stories of great tests of faith as well. We will today consider the story of Lazarus, mindful that he rose from the dead, as our men from the sea. Jesus waits two days after he hears Lazarus is ill, and only on hearing of his death does He go to Bethany to meet the grieving sisters, Martha and Mary. When He arrives, Mary in anger confronts him: Lazarus would not have died had He been there, she weeps. When Jesus goes with her to the tomb, he too weeps. He weeps for his friend, and for the grief of his sisters. Where was God?

We ask that question today for ourselves and for our lost men. Perhaps the question we mean is not where was God so much as where is He. 'Where is God when it hurts?' Part of the answer comes from Calvary where Jesus dies with the other condemned men. Eternally inseparable from humanity, He dies right there with them. And the other part of the answer comes from each one of us ministering to others. God is there with us—binding wounds, searching, bringing the lost men home, comforting the grieving, offering food. We are looking after each other as best we can—eternally inseparable.

Let us go in Peace. Amen.

...---... ...---... ...---... ...---... ...---...

N S in distress; want assistance

      in distress

      want immediate assistance

Q J I am sinking

      send all available boats to save passengers and crew

Q U have no lifeboat

      have no lifeboats here

U P considerable sea

U Q heavy sea; much sea

U R much swell on

U V too much sea

Y E want assistance

Y G want a boat immediately

Y J want immediate assistance

...---... ...---... ...---... ...---... ...---... ...---... ...---...

The *Budding Rose*

C X no assistance can be rendered; do the best for yourselves

N R I will not abandon you; I will remain by you

When Mrs. M comes these days, she has nothing to say. She just sits and looks. Morag, I can hardly bear it. She is so dispirited she doesn't even talk. But didn't she see me coming up the road in the gig, then, and wasn't she here before I had a foot on the ground! Wanted to know why are we home in the gig, and me struck dumb with the hat. Phemie, bless her! Phemie was out the door, steering Mrs. M away home like a stray nanny goat, before she had time to say aye, yes, or no. So, I was spared for the moment.

THE WRECK OF THE IOLAIRE.
55 WIDOWS AND 204 ORPHANS
STORNOWAY 9 JANUARY 1919

I have now ascertained the full effect of the disaster to HMS Iolaire, which floundered on the Beasts of Holm rocks when entering Stornoway Harbour on New Year's morning, with some 300 Navy leave men on board. As far as can be gathered, 174 men lost their lives, and of these 55 were married, leaving widows with young families, while one was a widower with four children. In many cases the widows have from four to nine children to support, the total number of children who have lost their fathers being 204. The disaster has affected the whole community of the rural parts of Lewis. Over 60 villages are affected, covering a distance of 60 miles from the Butt of Lewis on the north to Breanish on the borders of Harris, and even the adjacent district of Harris is affected, as out of 12 naval men from there 6 have been lost.

At a joint meeting of the Lewis District Committee and Stornoway Town council, EX-PROVOST ANDERSON, chairman of the District Committee presiding, it was unanimously agreed that, in view of the wide-spread sympathy felt for the bereaved families, respectfully to ask the Government, through the Secretary for Scotland, to arrange to hold as early as possible a public independent inquiry into the cause of the wreck and the great loss of life which ensued therefrom.

… holed up in his room in town, his people's goin' t'ither and yon, an' our men drowning. What was he doin'? Four hours for first-aid equipment. What were they doin' any of them? No lifeboats. No horse. No first aid. No transport. No nothin'.

Useless, the lot of them.

… they found the Captain right over here, by the wall, dead as a mackerel … two lifejackets, for all the good they did him.

… No. No. His body was never found …

They said the telegraph man washed up, with a piece of the wireless still in his hand …

… moved up to Vice-Admiral he is, the day before the inquiry comes out in the papers, and in onto the Retirement List the very same day. He'll be Prime Minister next.

i. *Iolaire* passed the lights at Arnish Point and Tiumpan Head.
The Ratings were getting their kits together and getting ready
to land when she struck.
Some could smell land.
She listed in maybe ten or fifteen minutes.
The seas came breaking up over the deck.
Men jumped overboard.
Men were washed overboard.
Two sought refuge up the masts.
One got thrown off when his mast snapped, the other clung
to the mainmast for more than 8 hours. First the ship was
bow to the land but then she lifted and went stern-first and
broadside.
The sea was rough and lifeboats swamped.
One man got a rope across to the rocks and held on for others.
When the rockets fired the lights showed the rocks just a few
yards away, 20 at the most.
Men were jumping to try to get to a rock ledge that was closer,
but there was a very strong current. The rope strung ashore
went slack and taut as the vessel swung in and out.
The rope saved 79 and jettisoned others before it was lost to
the force of the floundering ship.

ii. It was a fine night, clear weather, a breeze astern—
southerly wind.
It was a very stormy night—a hurricane of wind and rain ...
The night was very dark and there was a heavy sea running.
I wouldn't say it was a *stoory* night.
Stormy and wet, it was. There was a big sea running, and the
wind was increasing all the time.
I would not call it a gale. Just blowing pretty strong. It was a
bad night ...
Welcoming the New Year—a special night it was.

I wouldn't say it was a stormy night.
The sea was pretty heavy.
It was a squally night—a hurricane of wind and rain ...
Blurtin, it was. There was a big sea running. And the wind ...
the wind was increasing all the time. I would not call it a gale.
Just blowing pretty strong. It was a bad night ... weatherful.
The night was very dark.
... and there was a heavy sea running.
The glass was rising, they said—
There'd be no glass rising on a night like that.

I didn't have a good fire on today and it's gone cold and awfully dark for only half-two. And wind! It's his name in the hat, Morag, but if I ask, 'Is it his?' they'll just look away. It's not that there's just one Murdo MacLeod, is there? But where is my Murdo do you think? Morag, I should have just left it there to the waves. But it stopped. At my feet. It came to me.

Whenever Himself is home, in comes the cat and she finds his hat every time, and she flips it over and drags it around, and then climbs in and curls up and off to sleep she is. But she's too big, and there's always parts of her hanging out. Remember the postcard, how he named her? Bast. Egyptian war goddess, protector of the home front, it said under the picture. 'Good ship's cat,' he said. 'But all the better here.' Fierce and scrapping she was when he found her half-starved in a crate. He got some milk into her, then he put her in his hat, a bit of towel to tuck her in, and left her near the warm fire, same as the pet lambs. And pleased as a dog with two tails, wasn't he, bringing her home. She gives him a row, don't you know, when he needs the hat back—and she always wins. I can see him sitting here working his knots for her hammock. Him and his sheepish grin when he had to confess what he was doing—his eyes shining when he got it hung up for her. 'I want the two of yous waiting for me when I get back,' is what he said.

Now, don't you know, his mother has a soft spot for her too.

HM Naval Base, Stornoway.

8 January 1919

Sir,

We have the honour to report that in compliance with your memorandum N.19/13, of 7 January, we held a strict and careful inquiry into the circumstances attending the loss of HM Yacht 056 'Iolaire,' and are of opinion (sic) that HMY 'Iolaire' stranded on the Biastan Rocks ... and became a total wreck.

There is no evidence to explain how the accident occurred as none of the officers on board, or the helmsmen or lookouts who were on deck at the time are among the survivors, and no opinion can be given as to whether blame is attributable to anyone in the matter.

The Court is further of opinion that no adequate or properly organized attempt was made to save the lives of those on board. The only steps taken were to fire rockets, burn blue lights, and blow the whistle to attract attention. The boats appear to have been lowered without orders or guidance ... (PRO 495, ADM 116, 1869. p 16).

They asked us to say and then we couldn't have our say. Was I on board was the first question. *Yes.* And where was I on the run? *On the boat, I just said that.* And what time was it when she struck? *I didn't think to look.* Where was I when she struck? *Still on the boat.* Where was I? *Just around Arnish Point.* Where was I? *On the deck.* Where was I? *At the rail. Standing at the rail.* What did I do when she struck, simply stand still? *Aye. I stood still. For a long time. I got over the side with a rope.* That was their questions, you see, and I had it in my head to say what happened. But that's not what they wanted. Where did I go after she come ashore? *Portside when she listed. To the lee side. Over the side. And the waves washed me ashore.* Did I see any officers? *I don't know.* Who did you see? *The lights went off. It was pitch black except for the foam. I was at the rail. I smelt the land, we were that close, you see. And I was going below to say, 'We're home, Lads,' and I heard someone say, 'We're too close.' And then she shuddered. And then the bell, and that's all I heard, just the bell. And then she quit. She all quit.*

It is DB in the dreams, the same as in Is's letters. In some trick of imagination, I am entangled with a character that did not exist except in spirit in 1919—then or decades later. But he does. He haunts me, this returned lover, with an intensity and purpose that I can neither shape nor hold in the story. In the aftermath of the sinking, Is gathers strength in keeping DB's presence alive to her, telling him what is happening in the village. He 'accompanies' her as she pursues the life they dreamed together, far beyond the Beasts of Holm.

A fortnight gone. I have a routine now. First thing before I'm even up, I tell myself, 'Today the hat goes back.' Then after my porridge when the light comes, I go down the croft to the sea. When I get to the sand-cliffs, I can't go one step farther, and I sit in the marram grass. The rabbits eventually come out of their burrows and the day wears on, Morag. I come in when I'm cold.

In Sandwich today, ten buried together. Known unto God. Is one my DB? The stream of carts bringing the coffins to the villages has stopped. People walk out a bit, mostly the men, but the village is too quiet. Lowered voices everywhere—in church, in the shops, at the post office, inside and out, even the children. Survivors cast their eyes down for mourners, for anger, all for sorrow. And DB?

HOW much easier it might have been for the people of the Long Island to lay to rest the tragedy of the *Iolaire* had there been formal charges of criminal negligence against the Royal Navy, or had the Royal Navy itself moved to accept responsibility for the disaster.

How relieving it might be for the people of Lewis and Harris to manage the tragedy, since they would never, finally, put the sinking behind them, generations numbed with a grief all the worse for the crass indifference. Crass indifference. How much easier for them to move on if the Lord High Admiral and the Sea Lords had simply remembered *The British Manual of Seamanship* dictum: 'Never overload a boat.'

Many did respond. In the aftermath of the *Iolaire* Disaster, individual naval officers of note sent condolences and donations to the *Iolaire* Disaster Fund, as did others from across the British Commonwealth and beyond. Decades later, in 1960, the locally funded memorial to the disaster was unveiled. In 1970, the findings of the Naval Court of Inquiry and the Public Inquiry were released to the public for the first time. A century later there is no sign of contrition.

... no opinion can be given as to
whether blame is attributable to
anyone in the matter.

It's worst in the morning when I wake. The bedroom is cold. I've been on the *machair* in my sleep, and it's as though I've come from the edge of the shell-sand cliffs on the *Tràigh Mhòir*. I've been looking out farther than I can see, to where the ocean doesn't end, looking toward home. I've been on the Island. I'm not here thinking I'm there: I know the difference. I'm *here*, with my thoughts in my *real* life supposing another life—other lives. The lives merge in a story about a boat wreck the year my father was born to immigrant Aberdeenshire Scots on a small homestead in Manitoba. It's the boat wreck that takes me *there*.

The ocean opens the divide—as does my father, gone. Loss is the real divide. My boat story would have meant little to him, displaced prairie boy who spent his working life in a smokehouse at the 'packers' in the city once known as the 'Chicago of the North.' The prism of time is less simple, perhaps, than the new grass in the *machair* or the ebb of the sea.

The *machair* at first glance could pass for Manitoba farmland with its own endless sky—but only at first. In early June, prairie fields are fresh green, but the *machair* is white with lawn daisies and bog-cotton flowers, wispy, wind-torn cottonballs all the whiter for the brilliant watercolour-blue sky.

She was bumping pretty badly when she first came onto shore off the rock where she struck. She came off the rock stern first and her bow came round and she sunk with her head toward the west.

The sea swept me off the hawser and then washed me ashore.

Some of those who tried to get ashore by the rope were flung off …

… She went down stern first to the shore.

Q. Was there any panic on deck?

A. Yes, a little after she struck.

Q. Men running about the deck?

A. Yes.

I saw rockets red white and green—sent up.

The Siren was blowing.

… We were expecting some assistance from the shore.

Q. Did you get any assistance?

A. No.

He's not in the mortuary. His kit hasn't washed up. But the hat—I don't know what to do with it. I don't want it. Can't seem to put it down. So I'm sitting here feeling the sea cold seeping into me again and I see him take the hat off the hook and put it down for the cat. See him sitting here tying his knots, hearing him hum. He was always humming. As soon as Bast saw the hat, back went the ears and there's the four feet of her up onto my knee to take a look, tail flipping back and forth, whiskers working in the bargain. But after a good sniff she jumped down and that was it. Maybe it's not his, Morag, do you think?

Even the fire doesn't have much heart. The winds are too much for it, too much for the house. There's too much cold. The rattling on the roof would still the dead. I'm cold at the heart, 'and I fain would lie down.' When I go out again, I will return the hat to the sea.

Mary sends cheerful words. Says when it warms up the Morisons will remove to the hen shed on their own place, and she says her house is feeling larger at the very prospect of not bumping into someone every time she changes her mind. You know how often that happens! Her garden will be the first one ploughed. She's planting for us this year, DB, so even if our boat from Glasgow takes till Christmas, there will be potatoes and turnips to see us through.

And listen to this: yesterday your mother was asking would there be room for the bodach's loom on the boat. 'If you take that,' I said, 'you'll be thinking to take sheep, too, will you?' You should have seen the look I got for my cheek, and this time, she was out the door and nary an 'I never' out of her! She'd have turned the broom on you for laughing— and me into the bargain.

Mo ghràdh ort, chan fhaic mi tuilleadh gu brath thu.

Only your Is.

p.s. I hope you won't mind, but I've packed your Princess Mary tin. What a thoughtful person she must be to have one of those Christmas boxes for every serviceman, and her photo, and a lovely little Christmas card too. And you! I still can't believe you sent the chocolates home in the box! (You still have her pencil, I hope!) x x x, Is

BOTH trains from the south arrive late that Old Year's Eve, 1918; overcrowded, and late. It has been dark for two to three hours by the time they disgorge their passengers into the rail terminus at Kyle of Lochalsh. Many wait on the docks to be ferried home to the Western Isles, almost 300 of them bound for Stornoway and over 60 tiny villages—Shawbost, Leurbost, Crossbost, Sheshader, Knock, Habost, Coll, Aird, Arnol, Tolsta, Ranish, Eorodale—sprinkled stars in Lewis gneiss and night. Royal Navy libertymen, they are going home, they say, going home, going home for the first time in the four years after fighting for George V and Empire under conditions they could not ever have imagined in places with names beyond Gaelic tongues.

Dearest Morag,

I should have sent this when I wrote it, but I was waiting on better news; waiting to burn the worry and send a different letter.

I've put the hat on the dresser, and I try not to look at it but I can hardly look anywhere else. I can see DB coming through and leaving the hat down so the cat will climb in. I've left it down too, but she doesn't go near it.

Today, I have no more news than yesterday. Ten days gone and still no word. If she'd knock it down or get into it, I'd know it is his ...

You will remember one of the psalms today in church. How can they be so old and stay just right?

> 'O Dhia, a ta mi 'g èigheach riut,
> dean deifir thugam fèin:
> Is tabhair èisdeachd fòs dom ghuth,
> tràth ghlaodham riut am fheum.'

> 'O Lord, I unto thee do cry;
> do thou make haste to me,
> And give an ear unto my voice,
> When I cry unto thee.'

Heart-banging terrors me awake. We're hit again or we've hit a mine. And I'm seeing this lad hunched, pulling his collar up against the wind. And it's me, the lad is. Hanging onto the rail, I am, and the waters slapping up and over the deck, and the boat listing to the lee side. The lad, he's thinking how're we going to get home now? And he thinks, *Give the old bitch the boots to start with or she'll take you at the same time.* And the lad ties them together and flings them into the dark, and he throws his kit after them. But he's let go the rail to throw the kit in and the water takes his feet from under him and slams him along the bulwark, lashes froth over him. And I see him again with his cork vest. And the lads are going off the deck in the flare light, and the bell ringing, and the steam whistle in a thin piercing screech … And the boat's rocking, up and down, lurching starboard. And there's the waves. 1 … 2 … 3 … And knotted round his wrist is a silk scarf, and he turns it to the inside, counting all the while, and his fingers play the knot for a minute. And it's my voice I'm hearing. *I'm coming all right, you old bitch, but it's a short visit. I'm taking Ailidh her scarf—*

I berthed the Sheila about 10:00 that morning. The Iolaire come in about four, half-four. It was no matter her giving the pier a dunt. You could see all the lights on the way into Stornoway.

Arnish, Arnish beacon, and Tiumpan, A' Chàbag . You could see them all. It was clear enough.

Tapping the pier, we've all tapped the pier at one time or t'other. But no look-out, that's a different thing all together. You always have look-out, and you keep watch until you're in, never mind you've passed the lights or you're seeing the harbour lights. You could do without, but I don't know … It doesn't take much for-to get off course and land up where you don't want to be. Two or three minutes, maybe five would do it.

Myself, I had three of us on the bridge. Not the best night. Wet and stormy, that one was.

THERE were two yachts named *Iolaire*. Transferred to the Royal Navy by the executors of her late owner's estate, the smaller of the two, *Amalthaea*, replaced her duty sister and assumed her name in the darkening mid-October days before the Armistice. *Amalthaea* had known another life: in her saloons had hung portraits of Sir Charles Duff's Grand National Champions at Aintree in 1912 and 1913, the sway-back and ewe-necked Jerry M, and Covertcote. Her other life accrued mounting sadness. In 1914, Jerry M, the horse with the big heart was put down; Sir Charles himself passed on. In 1914, two bullets on a June day in Sarajevo changed the destinies of tens of millions. She carried home 284 Ratings on what would be her last run.

In the *machair* in late spring, the marram grass holds the pale gold of ripe wheat beside daisies smaller and closer to the ground than white clover. They thrive on sheep's paths along the sand dunes. Here, as in the proverb, I can plant my foot on nine daisies: *here* is spring. The young daisies turn pink when their rosy eyelashes close at sunset, but by day they blanket the cemetery in late-spring-snow-white. But for the dearth of trees, the daisies would scarcely be distinguishable from the ground-cover of faded cherry petals in the parks farther to the south.

Here, herring gulls and gannets ride out overhead turbulence, play the air currents. Young lambs frisk and revel in the spring as they do. They dive and peek round their mothers' shoulders, heads tilted as though to see from a better angle. They stand riveted, too, inquisitive, black liquid eyes following me from the grazings where clumping grass and marsh marigolds cover crumbled blackhouses, byres, sheds, and long-buried middens alike.

were you on board? *yes* what time did you go on board? *around 6:00* did you see the captain or any officers? *'find a place,' the captain said, 'make yourself comfortable anywhere—you can lie down on deck'* during the voyage where were you? *on the boat* were you there all the time? *i was until she struck yes until she struck yes* where? *on the deck* what did you do? *nothing* what did you do? *i stayed where i was* did you hear any orders given as to manning boats or anything? *no* where were you? *on the boat still on the boat*

what did you do, simply stand still? *yes* where were you? *starboard side at the rail* did you see any boat lowered? *no i was standing still* whereabouts? whereabouts were the boats lowered? *from the ropes* whereabouts were the boats lowered? *amidships* whereabouts? *for and abaft* whereabouts were the boats lowered? *starboard side* what happened to the boats? *i don't know they were crushed* were there men on the boats? *yes they were full* what happened to them? *they got crushed, thrashed out* are those the only boats you saw lowered? *i saw two* did you get in either boat? *no i was helping with the rope* were none of the ship's company in charge of lowering the boats? *no* where were the life vests? *on the skylights* where were the life vests? *in the boats*

did she simply hit rock and remain stationary? *she listed starboard* did she stay put? *no the water lifted her and swung her stern-round to settle* did you see any of the officers after the ship struck? *the lights went out* did you see any of the officers? *no i saw men* did you notice any panic? *no* do you know … *i don't know what time the ship struck maybe you would think to check the time* how did you land? *by rope over the side till i lost the rope and the sea washed me ashore*

Dh'iarr am muir a thadal—the sea asked to be visited, people are saying. The burials are mostly done with, and none in the villages any more. They bury the men closest to where they come out of the water, bury them by lantern light, bury them so the women won't see them, and they won't let families bring them home.

And it's gone quiet. No more carts squeaking on the road, not like at first. Worse, there's still men not found. We've all of us died some, DB.

I wrap myself in a wool tweed throw, sit in the window recess braced against the draft coming through every crack and crevice in the house, slant rain lashing, trying just as hard to get in. In those minutes of not-quite-sleep, after the wind-long night, rackety roof tiles, and rattling windows, I expect the aftermath of a blizzard at home. I come, instead, into Is's place through footfall past the house, cuckoos, assemblies of greylag geese, sheep and sheep dogs answering to the whistles. In the house the decades fall away and I think on the rhythms of waiting out night on night through years for men to come back from the sea. What it meant, to keep the home fires burning.

My Island 'whitehouse' it turns out, was built in 1923 by the brother of two lost seamen. It imbues me with the past, I think. I want to believe it suspends the present. I hang my washing on the clothes pulley above the peat and coal stove. I keep my butter and crowdie cool in the larder. I live in this house, I sometimes tell myself, with Is. I 'place' her kist to the right of the stove near where we set our boots to dry. I write from the wooden Orkney chair from the window side of the stove where I look to the road that Mrs. M beetles across from her blackhouse, the scent of peat swirling around her.

In dream or out of it, I am absorbed in a village that boasts a school, a *ceilidh* house, a historical society, churches, a cemetery, and a tiny community shop, (the) *Bùth*, that besides offering groceries and hardware, houses the post office where Dorothy franks the mail with a date-stamp she changes daily by hand, and in the windows posts funeral announcements and community events.

Iolaire she was, sea eagle, *iolaire sùil na grèine,* eagle with the sunlit eye.

Iolaire mhara (sea eagle), *iolaire chladaich* (shore eagle), *iolaire ghlas* (grey eagle), *iolaire bhàn* (pale eagle), *iolaire fhionn* (white eagle), juvenile-*iolaire bhreac* or *riabhach* (speckled eagle), *iolaire*: a name for memory.

Irony abounding—the boat named for the bird that foreshadowed war and disaster. *Haliaeetus albicilla,* its Gaelic name in the *Seann-sgeulachdan* (mythology): *fior eun,* the eagle, 'the true bird,' messenger for Zeus and Jove, icon under whose silver, spread-eagled wings and thunderbolt talons Roman legions marched.

The eagle still takes the weak, the unguarded (the metaphor inescapable)—takes the lambs.

For Caesar's cremation, the great bird's release (no phoenix from the flames); for Charlemagne, a symbol of war-torn-cum-united Europe; for the Vikings, an eagle on an ash tree, symbol of mastership and power, snake coiled at its foot.

It was said the eagle sharpened her beak on the 'fatal stone' before slaking her hunger on the bodies of slain warriors. The eagle, white-tailed eagle, grey-coated eagle—greedy war-hawk in the fields, it was said, when Æthelstan took the North and the Scots. *Theirs was a greatness / Got from their Grandsires.* Æthelstan long gone, the eagle fleeted to sea.

The *Iolaire* caused a tempest like no other. For the people of Lewis and Harris, *the slaughter of heroes hap't there, too.*

19 days and the news comes in waves. 200 men, Morag—Shawbost, 9 lost and 3 saved; 5 on board from Laxay, 1 lost; 5 from Shader; from Crossbost, 3; 2 brothers from Gravir, 1 lost, 1 saved (Jack's cousin George); from Arnol, 4 lost. 11 lost from Tolsta, 2 missing, 5 saved; from Sheshader, 10 lost. Newmarket, Stornoway, 6 from Harris. Why were they even on the boat? The list goes on. 200 men lost, some saved, Praise God, but DB?

Tha mi sgìth 's mi leam fhìn.
I am tired and I am alone when I do cry to Thee.

The September morning at home matches the temperatures of my Island house and takes me there, where *caorans* fetched in before the rain coax peat and coal to start the boiler. I have learned to set the dampers and to rattle the embers in the firebox before they go cold. I didn't just burn the peats. I went to the peat banks to help with the second lifting, trundled some in the wheelbarrow to slow the diminishing of the stack in front of the house. A sense of guilt accrued with each scuttle of peat I brought inside. I increasingly used coal delivered from town, rather than the peat-store kept for someone else's winter. I developed a small sense of the labour that purchased the peat I burned.

In attending the Rayburn I recovered my Father's rituals. I could hear him shovelling in the dusty basement coal bin in the 1950s. His father and mother had banked night fires with wood to staunch the bitter prairie cold. Their parents in the Scottish Highlands lifted the peats, as do crofters on the Island, still. The echoes of our lives.

His mother sent him, about tea time it was—my grandfather—to fetch his sisters home from helping his older sister get ready for her man come home that night. Making some shortbread and scones, they were and what-like, you know, to make a special welcome home. After all that time worrying you see, everyone waiting for the lads, and what a time was planned. Life was going to start all over again just the minute they got off the boat.

Now, at that time of the year it gets dusk in the afternoon, and if you're going to be seeing anything, that's when you'll be seeing it—at dusk. And that's when he did—he saw the stag, him and his sisters. Standing in the path in front of them, it was, and it turned its head and it looked right at them, and then it was gone. So here's this young lad, big-eyed running in to tell what he saw, and he was about seven at the time, mind, so you can imagine the looks they give one another, and the sisters just kept quiet, now.

Well, he said at first they didn't believe him, and then, then they're asking what'd he done to be getting its attention like that? You know, you'd only see the white stag for two or three reasons—if you'd been doing something bad, and God sent it to warn you was one. But the other reason, and this one would be first to mind and last to come out, was someone was going to die. And sure enough, the boat wrecked that very night. The sister's husband, he was lost, and some of the neighbour lads, too.

I haven't heard tell of the white stag I don't think since. There's no explaining it, is there? She just went down. Just like that.

A parcel in the post today, Morag. Not DB's writing, but it's from him. 'Watch for a parcel,' he said in his last letter, 'I got you a present.' Just like him, he didn't say what it was. It's a sweetheart pin, Morag, in the shape of a crown, well, the part of the crown that would sit to the front of your head, anyway, and there's two wee sails unfurled on either side. And up at the top, two tiny pennants and all over, sparkly diamonds. And a silk Christmas card, embroidered, 'To My Sweetheart.' He didn't write on the envelope, either. The hand is small and neat and slopes backwards. I don't know what to think. I've been so worried if it's his hat, I forgot to worry about anything else.

Chan eil mo shùil ris a'mhuir.
He won't be back.

no time for a rhyme to soothe or distract

    no time for words on deck   none from below

        no sweet Gaelic *fàilte* to calm the last longings of the heart

    the Beasts ripped into the side of the boat sea-lifted a-ground

        lifted and stern-sunk turned broadside to the rock-tooth Beasts

    no order   no time   no word no rhyme

        nor reason for the blue men, for *these* of all relicts :

of Jutland, the Dardanelles, Gallipoli, U-boats, submarines, destroyers, mined waters, sunk trawlers, prison camps

    these the King's men in blue

    barefoot, booted, bedeviled, be-doomed   who could know them in the dark

    blue men in the dark, heaving and boat-forsaken-voices calling

                another   and another   *just you drown me now,*

                        hear!   *and hear what I call you*

Answers

I was in the saloon, sitting at the fire. The Engineer Lieut. came in and told me to keep coal on the fire, and the next thing, I had my boots off and I just made for it. Up on the bridge I was thinking if it was ebbing and the boat remained fast, we would have a chance …

There was a man told me try working the search light, but the dynamo was broken. He was sending up rockets with a very pistol.

There was no confusion on board through men not understanding English.

In deference to the Rayburn, I timed my trips to town, hoping to return to a still-warm house on a cool day. Or I tried to. Sometimes neither *caoran* nor wood kindling could coax the firebox into life. Far easier, I discovered, to keep a fire on than to start one in a cold stove. No fire in the stove, no warm boiler, no heat in the house, no hot tea: cold hands, cold feet. A moral there for a sweetheart. When I was in better accord with my stove, I answered her silent invitation to cook and bake, the hot oven at the ready. Is cooked: so would I. Scotch broth with local lamb, and stock from the bones of a roasted chicken bubbled on the cooker. Apple and marmalade bread puddings, oatcakes, shortbread, and biscuits—crisp-topped and tasty as never before by my hand. The perpetually hot tea on the cooker seduced from me the baking of mixed-fruit tea scones. The scones I made after my stay on the Island were the same as any I baked before I left—a composite of flour and milk dried into hard lumps that not even melting butter or Tom's fresh red currant jam could improve. The scones stayed behind with the cooker and the friendliness of tea. They waited for the neighbours calling in on a walk by the house.

In Island tradition, Tormod left fresh herring for me the day someone brought him some. John A brought me fresh eggs; Tom, his berry jam; Kate, *Cullen skink* (with dry clothes after I fell into the bog); Steve, salmon *en croûte*. And the loneliness felt by exiles from time to time became mine when I returned home.

Four years in the Royal Navy without a word of Gaelic, and they said at the inquiry there was chaos because we didn't understand. That's what they said. And all the Island men stood up there and every one of them said there was no chaos. And there wasn't. You wouldn't think a thing like that would be quiet, but it was. The whole thing moving like the silent pictures. And we let down the boats ourselves and they threw us out and crushed men in the rocks.

And there was no officer on the bridge.

And there was no one in command.

There were no officers anywhere. Who would give orders?

2:00 PM

'Never since the great drowning has there been such a day.' Never could there be another.

Be warned, you'll want none of this. The Inquiry's done with, and even the light that was left us has gone out. All the women dress in black now all the time, and no one would dare not. DB, we are black from the inside out, the outside in. Today now, it's gone even quieter—the quiet after we all heard. There's hardly anything to say. Two days for the Royal Navy Enquiry! People are waiting on a real one. I wrote down what the papers said from the two days: Iolaire stranded on the Beasts and wrecked. Well, you won't find a soul on the Island who didn't already know that, or in the Admiralty's fancy words: 'The deaths resulting therefrom amounted to 205 … our men drowned.' Whose men? My man?

The Rear Admiral regrets …

Na-a … what was he doing?

The Rear Admiral has asked …

He's asked, has he? No, it's us that's askin'.

We'll wait for as long as it takes.

And our sons'll wait after us, and their sons after them.

It's a cunning man what knows when to make himself scarce.

No look-out on the bridge! Nobody would come in past the Beasts without a look-out. And not a word to account for the boat ending up on the wrong side of them. Well, I can account for it. It was no Lewisman bringing her in, nor Harrisman either. And no, it was no 'failing'—just what the Captain and others bringing her in didn't do that any one of our lost men could have done blindfolded.

And this—DB, look at this: 'The jury desire to add that they are satisfied that no one on board was under the influence of intoxicating liquor.' In their stone heads, do they think it was tea put the boat on the rocks? And who did the jury think would say the Commander (or anyone else) had been drinking? The Ratings they didn't call to testify? Or the ones who are moving up the ranks? Not a word from that Admiral either on his useless life-saving apparatus, or on anything else, for that matter. He was safe enough in the hotel, wasn't he? And 3 to 4 hours to get the lifeboat from a mile away? But that didn't matter, they said. Because of the sea they couldn't launch it anyway. 'No opinion' can be given …

I couldn't read any more, DB, and I can't go on here, either. I've put the clipping in the envelope. You can read it for yourself.

A little Gaelic song for you before I go (and English, too) for those who pretend they don't need to know:

Teann a-nall 's thoir dhomh do làmh. Come give me your hand.

Teann a-nall, come to me, DB, thoir dhomh do làmh.

Your Is

QUESTIONS arise from the Royal Navy's cavalier indifference to Regulations, and the subsequent chain of events that began with the dispatch of The IOLAIRE from Stornoway to Kyle in the morning of the 31st of December, for the purpose of transporting passengers too numerous for The SHEILA to handle. Indifference to safety may have arisen from the exigency of the Royal Navy having previously made no arrangement for the final leg of men's trips home—servicemen weary of war and travel, arriving from London and Inverness heady with their liberty, disembarking at the railhead at Kyle, to return home on New Year's Eve.

There might only have been the best of intent in delivering the Ratings home to long-awaited reunions heightened by New Years' celebrations, and no less, the recent Armistice and the hope it engendered. Large numbers of libertymen came in on special trains that day. Additional transport for the Ratings from the railhead to the Western Isles should have been part of the transfer. Evidence has shown time and time again that consideration for Ratings is well down the list when it comes to the Command's convenience and expense. Seeing the men off to Stornoway, we propose, may have been more a matter of personal interest than charity in any case. Exigency arose, we charge, and with it anxiety in direct proportion to the numbers of Ratings boarding the trains to Kyle in the first place. It is common knowledge that New Year's Eve is not the time to press for abstinence on board ships or anywhere else, especially amongst men fatigued on many planes, men impatient if not utterly resistant to waiting ever longer for their much-anticipated welcome home heightened by the celebration of the first peaceful New Year's Eve in four years.

Fifty-one days since your last letter, and your beautiful silk hankie embroidered with the best words in the world: 'for my Wife.' Well, your wife keeps thinking, 'Just wait, he'll come home.' You promised, remember? I think maybe you weren't on the boat; maybe the hat is not yours, but Murdo Domhnall MacLeod's from Harris or Stornoway, or Eoropie, or Eorodale, or Barvas, or Point, or Laxay, or Lochs, or Lionel, from somewhere, and it's all a mistake. And when I sleep, your letter comes and I open it and silk stockings spill out. The kelp tangles on the shore and the stockings turn to red seaweed in my hands. And your breath is warm and sweet on my shoulder—your beard in my hair. 'I've a surprise, Is,' you say, 'Just wait. Just wait till we get to Canada.' And I will myself awake to cold and cheeks wet with tears. Oh, DB, Gur mise tha fo ghruaimean, I am in despair. What is to become of us?

Hearing Voices

MM: First, I would like to say about my mother. She lived to be 102, and her family—

CM: Her family, it was the same as ours, it was—two boys and four girls. And had she not been sick one time? And did she not hear the voices after that?

MM: Yes, the voices came after she'd been sick one time. She'd be about eleven or twelve at the time ...

CM: So sick she was, they didn't think she'd live, but ...

MM: Yes, yes. She thought she heard her sister cry out, but her sisters were gone to the herring, you know, and that sister, she was ...

CM: She was my mother's favourite, and she was the last of them to go.

MM: And she'd be about fourteen, I think.

CM: And wasn't she alone, then?

MM: Yes, yes ... and my mother was the only one left at home, then. And quite upset she was—was my mother, because she was the only one left you see, and she missed her sisters. Now her brothers, they were older, you see, they were in the Reserve, and they'd have been gone for a while. Gone away to the War, they were.

CM: And wasn't she gone to the herring?

MM: Yes, yes. I'll tell you about the herring girls now. You see, there wasn't much work in those times, and no work here for young girls. So they'd go down to get on as herring girls or maybe find work in one of the big houses in Stornoway, and they'd stay in town, you see, and look after each other. And that was where Mother's sisters was gone—

CM: To the herring ...

MM: So, my mother one day—my mother heard her sister's voice outside the house and went running, and, of course, her sister wasn't there. And later that night they came round, the other sisters was with them, of course, and told them she'd taken sick quite suddenly, and died the same day, in the afternoon ...

CM: And didn't she cry out ...

MM: Yes, and that's when my mother heard her cry out. There was a lot of people died like that, then. Now, I don't mind who all's voices Mother heard, but if I mind right, I think maybe the schoolteacher was another one. And I mind her telling about one of the young lads from up the road there that used to work for them while her father was away to the fishing.

CM: And they didn't believe it, her hearing the lad ...

MM: Yes. She heard him cry out, too, and he was gone the next day. I don't know—people was always dying like that. It was an awful time, you know.

CM: And she heard a voice that sounded like her brother's that New Year's, it was. And he'd been away ...

MM: Two brothers it was. They'd been away to the War, you see, and they was coming home with the other lads to the Island, and oh! a lot of goings-on there was, between the Hogmanay and the lads coming home.

CM: And they'd made the bannocks, and it was going to be quite a time, it was.

MM: Well anyway, they was waiting up the night, and she heard her brother cry out—just like she heard before ... And they were both—they never came home.

I am not fussed about the absence of a telephone in the house because there is a payphone outside the shop up the road. On a day drenched in blue beyond compare, even sun-bleached red of the phonebox makes the white *Bùth* brilliant white in the sun. The oxidized colour should have tipped me off. The phone doesn't work. No matter. No one uses it, I'm told. I bite my tongue, console myself with a teacake, and contemplate the forty-five-minute bus ride to town where I can use the Wi-Fi—in the library, the *An Lanntair* arts centre, the tea room, the pubs and restaurants. The bus takes me past the accoutrements of other urban centres: the fishermen's co-op, with outdoor gear for working fishers and walkers alike.

I walk from the entrance to the castle grounds along Bayhead, past the town hall and the harbour, where people waited for *Iolaire* on New Year's Eve. I walk on toward Sandwick, where Is and Phemie went on their first trip to town after the sinking. I walk where survivors passed wet and in shock, and I wonder that the lack of a telephone has put my feet on *this* ground.

In November, just after you left, I told you about the Armistice, remember? And you got so cross with me? Of course, you knew, you said, but you couldn't say anything. The censors would make puzzles out of your letters, blacking out lines until there was an empty slate, and nothing left that might give the game away to the Other Side. And think how cross you were about my next letter after that. 'Why don't you just send a postcard,' you complained, 'or perhaps not even write at all?' How to quarrel by post, DB: I am sure it's been learned or at least tried by far more sweethearts than we will ever know, and perhaps some of the quarrels were as innocent as ours for not knowing and saying, or knowing and not saying. And imagine you scolding anyway. This isn't a postcard, Murdo Domhnall, and you must know.

The Armistice is long past. You should have been here to see it—the Armistice, I mean. All white flags everywhere, white flags in the windows, on carts, bicycles, the postman's gig, and especially in the cemetery (!) though the ministers scolded us on Thursday, and again on Sunday—and that was fine. But here we are talking about the Armistice again. The minister told us there's to be five minutes of silence for remembrance. That seems the right thing, don't you think? Of course, some argue there's no need, how could we ever forget? The same ones argue no need for music, either, as though the Lord didn't give us ears to hear, or feet to dance, or dreams to dream, or anything besides the Book, and now we're left with little enough to do but pray. Well, the idea's got people talking, that's for sure. I wonder what you think. DB, where have you gone and got to? When will we dance again?

sorrow be my soul's crypt
sorrow the cold winter shore
sorrow the herring gull's cry

my heart a small stone
on the shingle
      cold and grey

I would cast myself
to the Beasts still warm with blood
I would fall into the sea
my blood to mix with yours

CORPSE CANDLES

Well, there's not been much talk about the sinking, now. I was just a lad five or six years old at the time, but I remember the night as clear as if it was yesterday. Mother had the tea on, and it was just getting dark, you see, and the dogs were going wild barking, and I was over to the window looking out to see what was wrong with them, and I saw some, well—quite a bit of light, it was. And it was in streams. Three or four streams to start with, and then in no time at all there were so many you couldn't count them. Like streams of sunlight coming in the window on a bright day, you know, only not so bright. More like light from lanterns, maybe. And they were in front of our house and my auntie's next door, here. And my sisters and I, we all went to see, and my auntie, she come along right behind us. Now, our grannie had been filling us full of tales about corpse candles, and what like, and you know about curious children.

Well, these corpse candles—you've heard tell of Will-o'-the-wisp, I'm sure. Anyway, that's what these lights put you in mind of. Well, the dogs were away across the road to the church, so off we went over there to have a wee look, too. And I said to myself, I said, 'Oh, something's going wrong here.' We thought maybe the minister was there and people with lanterns, you see, but there was no one there at all. Not a soul. And then the lights just went away—just disappeared. And we ran away back home in the dark not knowing what to think, you know, till the next day we heard.

I never saw lights like that again—just once, right before my gran died, just on the cusp of the night and just like those others it was, in the garden and across the road into the church yard again. And I followed them just like the other time. And that time I knew what was coming.

April 4

The sea is flat. The snowdrops and crocuses are out, and the days are getting longer. There's lambs, too, and I'm cheerier than in a long while—for now, at least. And I have good news. Well, it's old really, because I was saving to tell when you got home, but I can't keep it to myself any more. There's a baby on the way, Murdo Domhnall DB MacLeod. DB, yours and mine this wee one, in late July or August. And I haven't told a soul because I wanted you to be first and I've been waiting but, well, now that I'm not hiding under my loose clothing any more, someone else will be saying. I'd been thinking there was a baby for a while, but the nurse said it. She would be by, Nurse said, when she'd finished with Mrs. Morison, and I thought, 'What's she on about?'

Remember I was so tired there after you left? Maybe I didn't say. Didn't want you worried when you were needing all your wits to look after yourself, but most of all, I was waiting for you. Anyway, there's the other reason John Alick's coming to stay. I did tell you about John Alick? Aunt Mary's grandson from Ness? I went across to meet him at Dibadale, but with Phemie gone to Magaidh's we thought he'd best stay with your mother for now. She'll be glad of the company and the distraction.

On this September prairie morning, the wind serves a chill reminder of passing summer, and autumn arrives under sky dappled grey on grey. Only when the colour of the sky and snow match will the horizon disappear as it sometimes does on the Island in storm and calm, winter and summer alike. I thought I knew the sky, the vast open ceiling above the Great Plains, where millions of pinpoint holes sieve light through from the other side. I thought I understood 360° of sky where I can see every light in the galaxy, the whole swoop of the Milky Way, and sometimes the Northern Lights too. And, I thought I knew the moonlight. I did, until I saw it from the window of my house on the Island and saw the full moon for the first time. There it hung above the house across the road, turned spectral white against bright midnight blue, so bright it lit the path into the fishing lochs on the moor along the Road to Nowhere, pressed its big face right up against my window. I never went to the lochans at night, but Is would have, and so would DB. And sometimes the two of them would come back in the dusk of midnight, singing, the cuckoo still calling in the not-quite dark.

This night, I have been on the machair, this time, walking down the croft on the clumping grass and stones, beside the sheep and the fall lambs, and the neighbour's speckled and rust-coloured hens. Deacons, I thought—the three of them in a row, surveying their congregation on the Sabbath, on drought-dry ground. I don't know the croft any other way. In the silence of the *machair* and at the loch by the *Cala Ghearraidh* (Garry Beach), the sounds of greylag geese merge into the calls of Canada geese preparing for their long treks over my house. I see the cherry tree from the bedroom window, and the crows ordering the dawn affirm my place. These things here and there constant. When one recedes I will it back.

SURVIVOR ACCOUNT OF THE WRECK

I was working on the wireless when there was a lurch, and then another one, and everything went black. All I could see was the breakers cleaning the decks. Clearing off the men like flies.

After a time, I made it to the bridge. Like I said in my speech, the Navigator had lashed himself to the rails. 'It's abandon ship,' he said, and I—how long was I in the water, I can't say, but I got a good hold on the bottom of a cliff, the seas chasing me. After us all. And I'd climb up when the waves went back, and that's how I got up to the moors, pitch black in rain and sleet, and I thought I'd just lie down for a bit, but I thought the better of it. I fell across one fellow and got him onto his feet and we staggered together toward a light through the weather. The lad succumbed again, and I kept on going in fits and starts till someone helped me into the farmhouse and went back out to find the lad. They gave us a hot drink, and a farmhand brought a lantern to help us and found a handful of other survivors to shepherd to the Battery.

The Man of the Dream

By Chrissie MacLeod

My mother, when I was a lass waiting for my young man to come back from the War, my mother two or three times, I think, maybe three—I don't know just when—my mother told me she saw two lads standing beside me. Now, this was a vision, mind. There was two lads standing beside me on my left side, she told me. In her dream, this was. The one closest to me was my Alec, and she said I'd be married to him right enough, because if you had that vision that's what it meant. And the lad standing beside him, that was his brother, John, and she said I'd be married to him after Alec died, and it was bad she felt about that. And then, another time later on, she saw a third lad. He was standing closest to me in that one, and she couldn't figure it out because this time there was Alec but not John. And then after that awful—time—and Alec was—him and his brother was lost, then. I don't think she ever had a vision again after that.

You'll be wanting to know about the other man, though. Well, here it is. My auntie's husband was lost, too, and Mother helping out over there—this is just a day or two after the sinking. They just stayed down the road there. And she comes running, looking like she's seen the Devil himself. 'The other man's here,' she says to me, breath catching, my mother says, 'I says to him, "You'd know Chrissie's Alec, you would."' 'I would,' he said.

And she says to him, 'You'd be coming to see our Chrissie, then, would you?' And he says, 'Aye, Mrs. MacLeod, I would.' And there he was, right behind her at the door. And he stayed. And for the longest time he never spoke, never even told us his name. Oh, it was right after the boat, mind, maybe a day or two. He stayed up near Tiumpan Head. You see, he'd got safe to shore and got safe home all right, and then he come here. And he'd go down to the boats and go out with them. Every day, it's back and forth, and back and forth all the day, every day looking. Every day bringing some of the lads home, but never my Alec.

He come to help out, you see. He promised Alec he'd see to us if anything happened to him and John, and there he was. He'd be out at the boats all day and come in at night, and after the prayers and the Psalm, he'd just sit—sit into the dark, looking at the fire, looking out into the dark. The life was gone out of us, too. And in the morning, every day he was away to the boats—all the time looking for Alec, you see—six or seven weeks, I think it was, until they quit looking. And after that, Donald just stayed on. Oh, he'd hie away home every once in a while. He stayed in Ness, he did, but he'd be back in a few days. It was an awful quiet time. Whatever we did, we couldn't just … nothing was like it used to be. So many of them gone like that. And that's the way my life went, just like the vision, all of them gone now.

She used to wander up into the village and someone would see her and send her home like they did when we were children getting the messages, or someone would have to bring her home. Then she took to wandering in the moors. She never got over it. I got a little land in Manitoba and worked at that till the crops failed over there, and then finally, the grasshoppers got the rest. I was always going to bring her over, that was the plan, but then the War came again before I finally got back to the Island, she … Aye, that was a long time ago. My grandsons are that age now: Royal Navy Reserve, like the rest of us. They're good lads.

Na Fir Ghorm

Strange and frightening were the stories of *Na Fir Ghorm*, the Blue Men, who, flat-faced and fish-tailed, rose up from the caves beneath the waters of the Minch, close to Holm. It was the old men out fishing who first saw them floating in the cold sunlight of the Old Year's afternoon. The bodaich hurried in from the boats early, before the weather turned, to tell what they had seen and to see where their wives were, for it was the wives the Blue Men would be looking for.

The fishermen moored their boats and hurried up from the harbour. They spread the word in town and then warned their wives, but their wives told them to quit bothering them, and sent them back to tell their stories to the rest of the fishermen. Why didn't they fetch the fish they'd be wanting to go with the oatcakes for tomorrow? And the fishermen said nothing more about the Blue Men till they had time to sit round their fires on the Old Year's Eve, counting the hours till the new day. And then, the women still busy with the food for the next day, the fishermen talked quietly amongst themselves. There were too many of them, the fishermen worried; there was sure to be a storm. It was odd seeing them at all, there having been no sightings since the immigrant ship wrecked on the far side of the Island, far from the Shiants—the Blue Men and the SS Norge, in the wrong place at the wrong time.

They've kept Magaidh in Inverness, and Phemie's back to your mother's, so John Alick's staying with me at last. He's no bother, though it's strange having someone in the house again after so long. He's still missing home, away from his brothers and the bodach, but there's nary a word of complaint out of him. We're reading these days, he and I. The lad has his nose in the myths, he has, and into a book every chance he gets. We'll keep that quiet, too. At the rate he's going it won't be long before he's winning prizes at school, or in Manitoba if he comes along. Your mother was on about his staying with her again. 'What are you going to do when we're gone?' he said to her, 'Nothing to complain about.' 'I'll have to come,' she said, 'to keep you in your place,' and she gave him a cuff. Then he lowered his voice to confide in me. 'She's coming, you know. She just won't say,' he said.

Did I tell you Aonghas got back? He's having a bit of a time with a bad leg, but he's walking with two sticks and in good spirits, too—cheered by the fact that his one good eye now sees as clearly as it ever did, and that he was pronounced fit to come home at last.

And you, DB … ?

100 days. Tha mi sgìth 's mi leam fhìn. I am tired and I am alone. Tha mi caillte, I am lost.

Who was it said, 'Grief is no less for reason?'

Not a word to the minister now I've been writing a letter on the Sabbath, and setting a soot-black example for the lad into the bargain. I can't guess which of the two is worse, sinful ways or setting a bad example.

Aonghas Dubh came round yesterday with fresh herrings, and the lad was like a dog with two tails, but hadn't we just started to eat, when out he comes with it: 'Was it true—them being drunk on the boat?' My stomach went in knots, and the fire clicked and crackled, or it was maybe the clock or the sleet hitting the window, I don't know, till finally Aonghas spoke: 'Aye, that's what they're sayin.'

We've finished The Odyssey, John Alick and I, and, would you believe it, we've moved on to Shakespeare. We're making our way through MacBeth, reading aloud, yes, very quietly. I'm hoping your mother doesn't get a sniff of it, so you don't breathe a word. 'There's only one book anyone needs to read,' she'll say, 'and that's quite enough for my own flesh and blood.' And she'll be off. 'I never …' she'll say. Well, if she has a go at me over the books, you can be sure I'll be getting it all over again from the pulpit come Sunday. It's Catriona Mackenzie, I am, home from the herring with the red shoes her mother flung into the fire—after she tried them on. 'Jezebel shoes,' is what Catriona reported to me. 'Jezebel shoes,' the minister said. Heaven forbid they should know how I feel about silk stockings! Or you, DB, you'd be the Devil himself if anyone thought …

If it isn't fire it's flood. On Friday, John Alick took Topsy away to the shieling with Duncan, and it's rained the whole time. It's gone cold again, and windy, and then the light clears in the evening.

Always x x x x, Is.

In the deep night, the wind drives cold-thick rain into the windows, and I think of Iolaire floundering in the same wet black, and of the men shaken awake by her grinding and scraping on the Beasts. I go out barefoot in the dark and stand on sleet-flattened grass. The street light in front of my house has gone off and the snow-rain flies diagonal, horizontal, the light too dim for anyone to see a woman in a thin nightgown leaning into the wind. I am shaking from the freezing needle-rain driving into my face and my arms. Within seconds I am soaking wet and numb with cold. A few minutes outside, chilled through, I go back to the house, and I see someone else reaching to close the door.

It is as if I am watching, but I am dripping on the rug in a wet nightgown, hands and feet stinging. My hair has ice in it. I am here: not there. I am not watching, but I am seeing. There was a man in the shadow of the light as the door opened. He reached through the opening, reached for the woman on the threshold.

The shower coursing over me eventually drives away the chill and I wonder more who she is than he. And I see others: surging lost men rolling off the skewed deck, trying to hold onto railings, hands fumbling with rope, dark water, the noise of the breakers, the shifting boat, men numbed with shock and exposure, sucked under, men stumbling, scrabbling up the rocks through the whins, scraping and bruising themselves, staggering home. Not even the moon to light their way. The scenes run in a loop over and over the long night. They fade only as the wind and the wet snow stop, and linger in my dark thinking. What of the woman in the village where Is stays? Magaidh, driven to pick through the kelp for her husband's boots and never find them; Magaidh, bewildered, her blue hands, lips, blue with cold. Is going into the weather needing to know.

I have a dozen times passed by the Beasts of Holm hardly aware of the dangers of travelling on a ferry, but increasingly wary, nonetheless. I keep an eye out for the skerries, the Beasts. From the ferry, a spar that looks like a rocket rises from rocks in calm dark water. What do I know of the sea? On the land behind the Beasts of Holm the *Iolaire* marker points skyward. On the loose-stone path, I find on a memorial plaque the words etched in knotted rope on the brass. One image historical, the other more emotive.

OBSERVATION

Observation 1.

1. 24. (pg 25) CONFIDENTIAL RA Boyle, 14 January

... prior to the Court '... the following arrangements were made for collecting the evidence of the survivors from HM Yacht 'Iolaire':

> (1) Early evidence was taken from those who were in the Sick Quarters and those of the 'Iolaire's' crew who were survivors.

(20) All survivors were informed that their presence was required at the Base on Tues. 7 January, with a view to weeding out those whose evidence was of no value ... These amounted to 25. Those not required were allowed to return to their homes in the various parts of the islands. Some men were prevented from attending on medical grounds.

Observation 2.

> From the evidence there appears to be nothing to account for the disaster. No one of those on watch on the Bridge at the time are survivors.

> Ill-favoured rumours were circulated concerning the condition of the officers on board. These appear to have arisen from the fact that while berthing at the east side of Kyle Pier the 'Iolaire' collided with the pier. She was turning to berth with her head to the southward—a difficult manoeuvre at any time—sufficient allowance was set aside for the west going tide and the 'Iolaire' had rather much 'way on'. This was considered an error of judgment, and in no way carelessness.

Observation 3.

> The Master of the Mail Steamer 'Sheila' (that runs between Kyle and Stornoway) witnessed the above, and the above is his opinion of the occurrence. He also informed me that he saw libertymen, and considered she was handled in a most seamanlike manner.

> ... The Commanding Officer, Commander Mason RNR, appears

from the evidence to have gone below shortly after 1:00 AM on the 1 January, and Lieutenant Cotter RNR, appears to have been in charge of the ship.

Observation 4.

The large number of Ratings arriving at Kyle was unexpected. The 'Iolaire' had made two similar trips with libertymen during the first Leave, with Lieutenant FH Skinner RNR, in charge, and with a half crew. In view of the fact that the Ratings were looking forward to spending the New Year with such eagerness, it was natural for Commander Mason to take such a large number, although there were not sufficient boats or lifebelts to meet a case of emergency.

I was coming home, and I was going to get married, and my—well, these things don't always work out like you think. Mo ghràidh, you see, she lost her father and her two brothers and her two sister's lads on the boat, too. There was only her and her mother and sisters left. I was the only one come back. They'd look at me and see their own men. They blamed me for coming back. They didn't mean to, but they just couldn't help it. And sometimes I blamed myself, too. I was in line with the lads at the railhead. I should have been on the boat with them, but I traded for a place on the Sheila. I said to myself, 'You know, you left on the Sheila and it's right she takes you home.' The Sheila took me over and she was taking me back. Next time I went on a boat was the Metagama for Canada, I felt bad for going there, too. We all did. 250 of us, but there was nothing for us on the Island. The heart had gone out of the place. Things were just never the same.

The Sanitary Inspector has been round again. It's not a huge leap, DB, but they tell the children to wipe off the dipper before they take a drink, and that's it. They all use the same drinking cup and the same cloth. I don't think the problem's with the dipper or the cloth, or the children. The drinking water's not clean, and a flush latrine might make a difference. They could maybe use roof water, but try convincing anyone of that. In December, the school closed again but Katie's second girl took up the measles anyway, and didn't Dolina and young Calum take them, too.

There's another schoolmistress gone, and John Alick teasing me—I told them yes, I'd do it, but they're having someone from Oban. It's not me they want—I'm married, remember? (I do!) We can hardly blame Miss Cameron for leaving. Four children lost since she came, and her two brothers on the boat. It's too much. She's away home to stay with her mother. This, heaped on all the others—the Ratings, and now the children. Will it never end? 'Though waters roaring make, and troubled be … God strengthen us.' That's what we prayed in church on Sunday. Psalm 46. 'Oh God thou art my strength … I will give praises to Thee.' We prayed that, too, and I couldn't say a single word, DB.

Today arrived with promise: the sky and the water the same shades of blue. The snow's done, though it's still in the hills across the Minch. We're lambing. The machair is turning yellow with celandine and buttercups. I saw my first bonxie of the year wreaking terror on the terns at Tolsta Head at the weekend. I miss the rough of your tweed on my cheek, miss you smelling like a wet sheep when you come in. I wear your brooch always, even to bed.

Your Is

Iolaire sùil na grèine

sienna photos fade & release to light once-returning
    seamen   the Armistice behind with 18,000 at
Suvla Bay alone with St. George's Day at Zeebrugge Mole
Kaiser's hulks and minds plundered a generation lost to a war
fought in ways they could not have dreamt, spade in hand
cutting the peats on not-then so-barren Lewis
    Ratings   en route from Kyle   going home, going home

love is more thicker than forget
more sturdier than the slate-grey hull &
masts of the vessel *Iolaire*, more stronger than
proof of the Beasts of Holm waiting out the black night in the Minch
love is more louder than cries of drowning men   exploding boilers
    red filaments of distress flared across the New Year's sky
    till 20 yards from shore the Iolaire *sùil na grèine*   settled

    sunlight wrenched from eagle's weather eye
    back broken   19-pounder sunk
chart house, engine room wrested to the sea
hull and thorax offer no succor for *Iolaire*

We buried young Murdo Murray on his 8th birthday and Cirsty with him. She was 7. I don't know that Magaidh even knows they're gone, poor woman. She wasn't right, you know, when Murdo went back to Groningen, and then, you remember the nightwanderings. Sad it was to see Murdo and Cirsty hanging onto her for dear life after she'd been in the sea, and her fighting them every step of the way. It was better for a bit when Phemie first went to stay, but last night there were the two of them dripping wet over here, Magaidh shuddering in her shift and crying she couldn't find Murdo's boots. She nearly drowned the both of them. Just as well the children are away, and Murdo, too. Your mother was here with a dram almost before they got in the door, and John Alick with her. He went off this morning to fetch the nurse, and wasn't she already on her way here with a message from the doctor. They're just now gone off to Inverness at last, and not a minute too soon.

Goodness knows I can't say this to anybody else, but I wonder if we maybe shouldn't have just let Magaidh slip away to the sea. When she woke this morning, she cried and cried. She knew about the boat before it sunk. She told Murdo, she said, but what could she do? And then it was the boots in two straight rows, and the seaweed washing up around them, and the sea carrying them away, and the children picking bundles of wet black ribbon from where the seaweed was, but Murdo's boots weren't there.

Maybe if he were here things would be different. Maybe, if I just knew where you are, things would be different for me, too. I don't know, somehow Magaidh's story makes sense as time goes on.

The people on the Island, they helped each other through; they'd go and lay fires to keep the houses warm, and they'd take a little food now and again, the women would, and the men lifted the peats and looked after the animals to help out a little. There was always fish in the catch for everyone. People were looking after each other, you see.

And then came the Metagama and a bunch of us left, and after that the Canada, and the Marloch; it was endless. Not much work around; nobody wanted boats any more; the herring fishing was dead. People were fighting on the Island for land rights, fighting for land, fighting to stay alive. So we got our land elsewhere, and here we are now—able to go back and forth across the ocean without too much trouble—always on the wrong side of it.

I told you Magaidh and Phemie were away to Inverness, and they would have been, but for the sea. Today's no day to go anywhere either, and when they do go? We're hoping they'll keep her there for a bit. There's nothing for her here.

You'll think me foolish, but in my waitings I've come to think myself a Penelope, all fingers and needles. I've begun to knit a little on the front of your new gansey every day, and then every night before I go to bed I ravel out two rows (all 360 stitches). This I will do until I finish it, and I've promised John Alick one like it.

Well, that's the knitting. The letters I will just carry on. No need to worry, I'm still all right here on my own, and not to worry, either, that I'm gone daft on you. Daft over you, maybe. I write because it's like talking to you. It feels you won't be long back, and in the dark I wait for night to turn day and think what I am going to tell you next in anger I hardly dare put pen to, and I feed the words to the morning fire … DB, DB.

I have to go and ravel out my rows.

My love, mo ghràidh,
Your Penelope Alcyone Is

p.s. Look what I found in John Alick's book of myths:
The story of Alcyone and Ceyx. In the story, Alcyone walks on the beach, and her lost Ceyx visits one morning, and they hold each other once more, weeping, and the gods pity them and turn them into birds, Ceyx, gannet with head of gold, and Alcyone, kingfisher, orange and blue—and on seven days in winter light and on calm seas, when the kingfisher bird broods over her nest, the gannet comes to her once again.

I read *Iolaire*'s Captain's name on the plinth at the Portsmouth Naval Memorial and concede defeat. The words, 'In Memory of …' and 'Remembered with Honour,' reveal nothing more than I have found elsewhere. Richard Mason RNR I know only from what I found in accounts of the Iolaire Disaster. Some even have his name wrong. For another Richard Mason I could have obtained service records; could have found a list of medals, commendations, record of disciplinary matters. I could have confirmed the names of the boats he served on, and followed him on the seas to the rank of commander: all this and more from Admiralty archives at the Public Record Office in Kew. Of the Commander who took *Iolaire ex-Amalthaea* to her grave, I find only a wife's request to the Disaster Fund that grew from the sinking, she a woman with at least a widow's stipend. Most had not even that.

The single piece of information on the War Graves memorial reveals Mason was awarded the 'Reserve Decoration' (RD) by the Admiralty in recognition of fifteen years of active duty. The letters RD affirm the Admiralty's view at the Naval Inquiry that there could be 'no findings against such a man.' Neither would they brook any question about the competency of his navigational officer, Sub-Lt Cotter. The Admiralty appears to have closed ranks. Following the Naval Court of Inquiry, their Lordships of the Admiralty denied public access for fifty years.

I try to imagine Commander Richard Gordon William Mason and cannot. His body was never recovered. He remains shrouded and buried in Admiralty records, more lost than many.

Night-terror wakes me, my hands stiff, fingers numb with the memory of the iron-cold wet rails, the ache from hanging on. It's gone quiet. Something is wrong. My ears hurt from reaching into the silence and I force myself to stay awake for fear of being pulled back into the scrape-grinding, rib-breaking rock on metal, and the silence of black waves foaming black water across the deck of the shifting boat. Shock-cold water splashing over me, into me, and yet no sound with it. I know how it ends, this black and white movie, till my voice breaks through the membrane and jolts me awake before I become one of the dead. I've dreamed that too—becoming one of the dead—but sometimes I'm on the strand, dripping red kelp in my hands, or picking through the wet boots washed onto the beach, looking for the match to the one I have, looking for my hat in the sea tangle.

We were out to the peat bank yesterday but it was bad luck we had with the peat iron (the tairsgeir, John Alick insists). Oh, DB, we broke the handle! Mrs. Maciver said we should have soaked it first, scolded me for my carelessness. And I knew, because you reminded me before you left, but I forgot. And it's too late now, isn't it? She might have said something before it broke, I thought. But I said nothing, and you may congratulate me on my restraint. John Alick did. At least we got some work done before things came undone.

Aonghas Dubh has been fixing things again lately. He's better on his feet now, and hardly uses his stick. He was going to come today with the trap, but we convinced him to work with your mother in the lazy beds and let Phemie come in his place. He was away to Aberdeen again last week and still has to watch for his eye. He told John Alick he had his eye out for him, and the two of them laughed like maniacs. But isn't he looking and sounding himself again. Not to worry, DB, we'll have peat for the winter.

It's Saturday, and the tairsgeir is better than new, and the lad beaming with pride. He fixed it (with Aonghas helping, of course). So while they are busy fixing things, I am busy feeding them: I haven't made so many oatcakes since before my brothers left for Canada—surely, a lifetime ago. It seems they haven't gone unnoticed, DB. There's a bit of a competition started. Aonghas is the beneficiary. He can't go out the door without some woman offering him oatcakes or bannocks. John Alick delivers ours, and stays to read (well out of earshot). And the other day, weren't the two of them heads together, puzzling over a boat they're working on for the lad. They'll have it out on the water before long. Aonghas talks of doing the same with you.

Oran Bliadhn' Ùire   New Year's Song

    Iolaire Iolaire
  the gulls cried over white faces
rank and file laid out on the shingle beach in the *n'er* morning
high lament piercing lament mile-on-mile the calm receding tide
the waves too spent with the weight of the dead

   the dead weight they brought in

  in this wide air

   : the gulls cry *Ee-yo-lair-uh*

       circle
dip   drift
  shroud   *Ee-yo-lair-uh*

        hù a hó seo Bliadhn 'Ùr this New Year's Day
      hù a hó
        this day

           unlike any other

An obelisk stands on a small piece of flat ground above the Beasts at Holm Point, wire fencing wrapped around the cement base, words freshly painted on cold grey granite a few yards from where men scrabbled off the sinking ship. The photo resists. I feel like an intruder. When I finally frame the shot the camera batteries have gone dead, as though I'm being given a message. I turn back, unsettled.

The plaque at the head of the path to the monument draws me in. A woman in the lower left hand corner, wind-blown, searches, one hand on her brow, a lifebuoy clutched to her chest, her gaze seaward. Her hope and her raw loss bound in a border of rope—a lifeline for some.

The woman's left hand makes its own gesture. A hand on the brow might block light. It might block a view or shield the viewer. It depends where the eyes are cast. It is a gesture of intense thought, perhaps hope? Perhaps anxiety. Consternation? Despair? Fear. The woman looks out to sea in perpetuity, as the people of Harris and Lewis, the Long Island, have since at least the time of the Vikings. They have long looked to the sea for life, or a turn in their lives. But the woman gazes outward to the place of sorrow—*Biastan Thuilm*, the Beasts of *Home*.

Report not submitted

… blue flash caught my eye. Thought it was the Viscount's New Year's Eve bangers, nothing to worry about. The water getting up with the wind. Dark. No moon to speak of. A few fishing boats moving back in, people mostly away to their beds. Some at the pier waiting on the mailboat and IOLAIRE, come to finish and start the New Year. Come to see the lads home.

The pilot boat reported lights, too. I sent Wenlock back out on stand-by. He was still there at daylight.

Then I heard rumbling outside. I went to sort things out and there they were, five Ratings come out of the sea. Half-perished. Blue-lipped, stuttering cold they were, talking all at once, half-dressed, barefoot, wet through. Couldn't get much of anything, just words. The sea will take your words. Take your voice …

I brought them in, ran for some whiskey, rang my man. I had to hold the cup for the trembling—the trouble swallowing.

How many bloody times have I asked for supplies here? A few damn blankets. First aid. Everything at the Battery, and not even a motor car to get there and back. I had a driver but no vehicle.

… I would draw attention to the International Convention for the Safety of Life at Sea, 1914, with safety recommendations in the wake of the sinking of RMS TITANIC. Now this. Wireless wasn't working for months … men in danger from the outset. Lifeboats, vests, short crew numbers, no assistance … This will come out, and the press will be all over us. All over me …

A court-martial is in order. Inquiries have no teeth—no answers, no rulings, and there's no responsibility. There's no evidence of criminal negligence, no evidence. Everything's gone. Maybe error and maybe 'extenuating circumstances' in the mix.

People celebrate New Year's Eve wherever they are.

We got down there with the LSA and we couldn't find the wreck, so up to the farm it was, to see to the survivors. Some poor lads had got that far. In the morning when we could see, there were Ratings and kits and boots in the kelp and all over the beach.

1 Jan. 1919

1:50 blue light flares
2:10 message arrives asking for the LSA (Ainsdale)
2:20 red light flares
2:30 ship found in distress
3:00 message arrives asking for the LSA (Barnes)
3:10 LSA ready to go; someone goes to fetch 2 carters and their horses
3:30 1st carter called
3:35 2nd carter called
3:30 wrecked Ratings arrive to report to RAdm
3:40 RAdm arrives at the Battery; Coxswain and 3 men are there, and later joined by 19 more
4:00 LSA cart leaves
4:30 Murray reports to the RAdm at Headquarters
5:00 LSA can do nothing. Nothing to do: it's all over
6:00 Murray gets the mailcar
6:20 at sick bay to collect Surgeon Owen and attendants
7:50 1st aid, stretchers, arrive at Sandwick, still pitch black

... all the palaver for a public inquiry when ours wasn't good enough.

There was no wrong-doing, but that's not surprising, given the questions to the witnesses.
If the people had an agenda, so did the Royal Navy, make no mistake.

... should have been a court-martial to put things to rest
... and 25 depositions wrapped up in a day.

Some of the lads had to be helped into the room, and God knows, could hardly talk any more than the 5 that turned up at Headquarters.
... one cock-up after another from the start, and no one accountable because there were no officers alive to give an account. Can't blame them for thinking it was a whitewash.

... ran into the pier at Kyle, all right—no damage done. It's tight getting in, and here's a current.
... Many a boat's made safe harbour fortified by a good tot or three.
... the deponents all said there was no drink, but getting on the boat and getting a nod from the Captain—they wouldn't get close enough to know. The rumour's not going to go away.
... some of the lads at Kyle were waiting from the day before: they were wanting home.
The Red Cross hut was full up. I had the biggest boat and the closest available, for God's sake, I got them home, didn't I? Boyle got them home.

We had Aonghas Dubh's pony at the peat banks again yesterday, and we must have been too pleased with our work, for hadn't we just nicely finished our cruach when it came undone. The lad pulled at one turf sticking out and down came the whole works, Jericho without the shout. The lad looked more than a bit sad, and I shouldn't have laughed. I couldn't help it. But then when we were having our tea, he said his piece. I didn't build the cruach right. 'Next time,' he said, 'next time we'll do it the way … we'll do it tiled and flat, the way my mother … ,' and his voice trailed off. 'Aonghas and me will do it,' he said. And his eyes got bright and wide holding off the tears. 'Long and thin works better,' he said. 'We'll do it my way the next time.'

You know, I was thinking the lad looked an awful lot like you when the cruach came down. It's that look! Remember, I said you reminded me of my grandfather the time his watch fell into the bonfire, and he danced a jig with his rake trying to get it out, but the fire was too hot. You never saw the old bodach move so fast in all your life, unless he was at the ceilidh house and Donald Mòr playing too fast for his feet, or he was skipping away on the run from old Mrs. Murray's broom, him home singing and hardly able to stand up, him or Aonghas Òg, either. I got in trouble for liking the story! 'Time waits for no man,' he'd say, wiping his tears, laughing. 'Nor woman, neither.' And what did he need a watch for anyway? He knew when to go to bed and when to get up, and when to go to church, when to read the Book, and when to eat—what else did a man need to know? But the look on his face, him just standing there with his bare face hanging out trying to figure out what to do, and his watch in the fire—that was the same look. And then he'd say the watch was no good anyway; never did keep time. He'd thrown it into the fire on purpose. 'A man needs to set aside earthly vanities,' he'd say, and then my grandmother would give him a row all over again. It worked when she gave it to him, she'd say. Or she'd scold him for telling stories at her expense. 'I never thought I'd live to see the day,' she'd say.

Remember?

NOTHING is to be written on this side except the date and signature of the sender. Sentences not required may be erased. <u>If anything else is added the post card will be destroyed.</u>

I am quite well.

I have been admitted into hospital

$\begin{cases} \textit{Sick} \\ \textit{Wounded} \end{cases}$ *and am going on well.*
and hope to be discharged soon.

I am being sent down to the base.

I have received your $\begin{cases} \textit{letter dated} \text{_____}. \\ \textit{telegram " } \text{_____}. \\ \textit{parcel " } \text{_____}. \end{cases}$

Letter follows at first opportunity.

I have received no letter from you

$\begin{cases} \textit{lately.} \\ \textit{for a long time.} \end{cases}$

Signature $\Big\}$
only.

Date _____

[Postage must be prepaid on any letter or post card addressed to the sender of this card.]

I've packed and re-packed my things fifty times, Morag. We'll be on the first boat in the New Year, and Mrs. M with us! She's in and out of here crying and girnin a dozen times a day, knitting and a big stock of 'nevers' in tow, tailor-made, bless her! For the leaving: 'I never thought I'd see my children turn their backs and leave their own mother, and the bodach not cold in his grave.' (Six years!) For the peats: 'I never thought I'd see my peats in such a state.' 'I never thought I'd see your mother raise a girl who can't manage a cruach, not even with Phemie and Magaidh to help.' For me she never runs out of scold: the fire's not right, I'm wasting the peat. The house is too cold, my scones too dry, the soup or the porridge too salty, too lumpy, too thin—and not a day missed since Phemie's been minding Magaidh Morison.

I know she's done when, teary-eyed for my benefit, she takes her kick at my kist, my 'Canada trunk' I call it for her benefit. I've been trying to help her see, God willing, that we are going. And then she's away home with the cat. I asked her the other day had she started packing yet? Well, she hied out the door like a Ness sgoth in a gale, and not one man, never mind six, to get her launched.

Aonghas insisted on me riding in the trap yesterday for the Peace March. He's been pretty watchful, lately. He's kind like that.

Now, you're not to be alarmed, but there's two lads here now. The young one came on the full moon—our Lammas baby. He looks like you without the big ears, yet. But he's got your eyes, and baby eyelashes starting just now to appear, and his hair is all wavy. And he's loud, outraged when he hasn't been fed even before he thinks he should have been, and then he makes little chicken sounds. And he snuffles. He curls right up into me, tucks his little legs under him and makes himself into a wonderful fine little bundle that fits just right into my shoulder, inside my shawl. We'll wait on his name for a bit, give it to him on your birthday, maybe.

I've decided to finish your gansey so I can start one for him. It's kept me going, DB, hope in every stitch. Sometimes I've hated it, though. Hated it wasn't finished. Hated you weren't wearing it. Hated you were never going to wear it any more than you were going to wear your shroud. Hated you for not coming home in life or death. Ràn na mara. Of the cry of the sea, there is no end.

I have to turn and finish the neck—and then what? I'm running out, DB. Running out.

Forgive me, Is.

the tide bell rings

and I call for you in the heather and the thrift by An Cùl Beag
in the low tide from the caves from the
shadows of the stacks at Cala Ghearraidh
I call along the endless length of the Tràigh Mhòir,
beneath the slopes of the sand-cliffs, the scarred hills,
the tide pools; from the red seaweed I call
from black-sinewed strand where in grace in death gannets lie
feathers spread as though in flight, their eyes and bones picked clean
and burying beetles labour their days

I call from the blanket bogs, through the mists and the wind
from the shelter of the marram grass
where summer blues the forget-me-nots on the machair
where the greylag geese and hoodie crows, and
the ewes call in their own
so strong the pain of separation

The Gazette printed the King's proclamation for the first 'Remembrance Day,' Morag, and wasn't Mrs. MacLennan on about it in church. There she was waving her letter from the King. Again. His Majesty commended her on sending him all her sons. Remember after William went? All the King's men, she said, her seven all gone now, the last two of them on the Iolaire and her sons-in-law, too. Not even a black-edge telegram for the last two, poor woman, and nary a word from the King now they're all dead. 'There'll be none of your "remembrance" here,' she said, 'for the War Lords to hold over us.' Aonghas came down and spoke soft words and the service went on. Now, you'll guess the headline in the news today—'No Remembrance Here.'

The corncrakes are back, and the cuckoos, and the greylag geese, too, squalling and organized for the summer on the machair. The fire's gone down. My lads are asleep, but I sleep less and less these days as light slides in early in the morning and stays later at night.

Love, Is

Everything was to stop at 11:00 AM for two minutes, and it did—to a great, awful, grinding silence. Baby and I walked out to the Remembrances. In the aftermath it's gone rainy and cold and the day is gone flat. Well, maybe not: it started that way. The weather's no worse than it's been up until now. For three weeks, the boats haven't gone out. The storms have got the crops, so it's not looking good for the hay this year. There's trouble over land rights at Gress. There'll be no work soon.

Your mother—bless her!—has quit kicking the kist when she comes to check on us. Baby makes her forget. He's a strong Laddie, this one. Holds himself up already, and he's hardly wobbly at all. You should see him. He looks like you when he's cross and his forehead goes all wrinkly, but the rest of the time he looks like himself. On your birthday I gave him your name, as I said I would, but I can't bring myself to use it yet. 'DB' he'll be when he can fill your boots.

x x x, Is

Ciamar a thilleas dòchas … How can hope return?

Her last morning in the village, I would have Isabella take DB's fishing gansey from the stool by the fire, slip it on over her linen shift, and slide her bare feet still warm from her box-bed into the boots that have remained under the stool since DB last set them there to dry. I can see this in my mind's eye: 'You leave those boots right where they are,' he would say to her. 'I want to think of them and you on that stool just like you are right now looking at me looking at you looking at me. And I'll be the happy man with the two things a man needs most in the world—his girl and a good pair of boots. But, if something happens to me, Is …' Isabella would look away. 'If something happens to me, Is,' he would say again. She would pinch her nail into the loose skin at the base of her thumb, pinch so hard she couldn't cry.

'Is, you listen to me, now,' he'd insist. 'When Aonghas Dubh gets back all right, he'll be needing a good pair of boots, too.'

'Your socks,' she'd say through a voice that wouldn't work for her. 'Did you—?'

'Is—don't you be going to waste either. Aonghas is a good man. You tell him I sent you.' He would turn away from her and stand, silent, looking out the window to the sea, his voice with no more strength than an old man's. 'Promise me, Is,' he'd say. And when she wouldn't answer, he would clear his throat again and, barely whispering, repeat himself. 'Promise me that, Is, before I go … Promise me …'

Isabella wouldn't hear him for the throbbing in her thumb, wouldn't hear properly. 'DB's voice,' she would think. 'He's not saying all the words. Something's wrong. He's missing words.' And she would pinch still harder, till she drew blood, and think, 'I've broken the skin.'

When we next see her, Isabella would not have moved; she'd have waited for him to turn back to her and speak again. But he'd have put on his hat, picked up his kit, and gone out into the wet dark of the morning. And when the grey light came to the day, we would find her still sitting on the stool—dry-eyed and mute as when he had left.

We would watch her make her way through the all-but-moonless dark to the sea that last morning. 'I didn't answer. I didn't even answer,' she would think, and she would see little in the dark, and hear only the sound of the heavy boots scraping and clumsy on the worn path to the beach. She wouldn't register the sound of the surging and ebbing water or the shore birds already into the day. She would hear nothing. She would sense the words in her head wresting free of her hold after months of waiting to be said when her man came home. But they would be trapped inside till the moment the sea took them, and there would be nothing. Only the sound of the sea.

On her last morning in the village. Isabella would put on DB's new gansey over her shift, clutch it to her, and walk barefoot in his boots, down to the sea. She would stand at the edge of the receding tide watching the sea and counting the waves coming in. 'They always come in threes,' she would tell herself. 'That's how some survived, because they knew that'. And DB—DB knew that, too.

Knowing she has a favourite place to go, we might imagine her there that last time, but not for long. The chilling fog is worrying the spring night into day, or not lingering perhaps. She's just gone to say goodbye. Certainly, by that time she would have left off writing her letters to DB. The gansey and the boots we know from the letters, some even begun when, heart-sore and grieving, Isabella went off on her own to watch the seaweed rise and fall with the edges of the waves on the beach, and to stay and watch the sand cover it and roll it in the wind. Or she would hold it in a dream and wait, but she didn't talk about grieving in her letters.

I'd like to think Isabella most missed DB when she woke up at night and couldn't get back to sleep. She would have taken as much comfort from the sheepy smell of the gansey as from its warmth. The boots are another thing altogether, having been DB's brother's. Murdo Iain (a Dhà), RN home on his last leave, passed on with his death. DB had insisted the boots would dance at his wedding, if not their owner. 'I'd put my boots under her bed any day,' a Dhà had told DB when he first brought Is across from Aberdeen, a comment given—and taken—as the approval DB needed before he asked Is to marry him.

I'd like to think, too, that Isabella would not give the gansey or the boots to the sea for DB, but would tuck them in with the books safe in her Canada kist to be taken out later, in a ceremony of beginning. I'd like to imagine as well, that on that same morning, she left for Manitoba with the baby whose name she couldn't yet say, with John Alick, and DB's mother and her loom and maybe even some of her sheep, and Aonghas Dubh, of course, all in tow. All this we might imagine if we don't let a search for history get in the way, for in the Killarney district of south-western Manitoba, or near Lloydminster, Saskatchewan, where there were two generations of Leòdhaisich and Hearaich to welcome newcomers such as Is and her family, there won't be found a trace of her or the land DB was keeping as a surprise for her. Imagining her leaving the village one way, we might have as easily imagined her, steady of step, leaving another.

i am herestill tonightseeing
moonmissing steady lifestep by step beside me

greytone till tonguenumb ebb to Aprillight
on sunspun moonset *machair*
springfused   grace in fitful return

alwayseye trained on moondancing neaptide
I wait life'swait on pink and marramgrassmoon
dunerustling sandstirring shinglesong
windcall's rise on seasglasscalm purplegrey to foralways

i
  hold you on the strand
   i in the bride-seat my longline fling
    plow your flit-boat where the seabirds fly low
       loose quavewaveringhope into drizzlesquall
         and therebreathe   thymescent
           roseroot in windsoughed grief
             and ply toward the headland

TIMELINE

31 January 1918—1 January 1919
1140: HMY Iolaire departs Stornoway for Kyle of Lochalsh
1600: Iolaire arrives at Kyle; bumps pier (no apparent damage to the yacht)
1930: Iolaire casts off for Stornoway
0025: Iolaire 12 miles from Stornoway
2155: Iolaire clears the North Point of South Rona, and thereafter alters course to North 2 degrees East until South East of Milaid Head
0030: Iolaire begins to steer North from North-easterly; beginning of squalls with drizzling rain
0155: Iolaire 20 yards from shore; fires rockets

GLOSSARY

Scots / English

bonxie	Great Skua, skua gull
bracken	fern-like moorland plant
Bast	goddess of warfare and protection of home territory in ancient Egypt mythology
byre	cowshed
Cullen skink	smoked haddock, potato, and onion soup
dunt	heavy blow, thump
gansey	seaman's knitted woollen sweater
glass	barometer
girn/in	complain/ing, grumbl/ing
lazy beds	parallel banks of ridge and furrow hand-dug with a spade
libertyman	a sailor on shore leave
marram grass	beachgrass on coastal dunes
rating	non-commissioned sailor
shieling	pasture for summer grazings
skerries	rocky islands (too small for habitation)
smoor	to smother
stoory	wild and stormy
tup	ram, male sheep

Gaelic

A' Chàbag	Kebbock Head
bodach (bodaich)	old man (old men), also spectre or ghost
bùth	shop
cailleach	old woman, wife, crone, hag
ceilidh	social gathering with storytelling, singing, and music
ceilidh house	private or public house that hosts a ceilidh
caoran	small crumb of peat
cruach	peat stack
daonnan	forever
dubh	black
feannagan	lazy bed
Hearach (Hearaich)	inhabitant/s of Harris, the southern part of the Long Island
iolaire	eagle

iolaire sùil na grèine	eagle with the sunlit eye
loch	lake or land-locked arm of the sea
lochan	small loch
Leodhais (Leòdhaisich)	inhabitant/s of Lewis, the northern part of the Long Island
mo gràdh ort	my love
machair	coastal habitat of shell sand, marram grass, and flora used for rough grazing
seanair	grandfather
sgoth	(Ness boat), skiff for fishing
tairsgeir	peat iron, spade for cutting peat
traigh mhòr (mhoir)	big beach

Gaelic lyrics / expressions

Tha mi sgìth 's mi leam fhìn,
Buain na ranaich, buain na ranaich
Tha mi sgìth 's mi leam fhìn,
Buain na ranaich daonnan.

I am tired and I am alone,
Cutting the bracken, cutting the bracken.
I am tired and I am alone,
Cutting the bracken forever.

'S bochd nach robh mi leat a-rithist,
Sinn a bhitheadh ceòlmhor;
Rachainn leat gu cùl na cruinne …

It is bad that I am not with you again,
We would be great music;
I would go with you to the other side of the world …

nam faicinn thu a' tighinn

if I saw you coming,

'S bochd an naidheachd 's gur brònach

Sad and sorrowful is the news

gur mise tha fo ghruaimean,

I am in despair.

Teann a-nall 's thoir dhomh do làmh.

Come give me your hand.

Teann a-nall.

Come to me.

'S thoir dhomh do làmh.

Give me your hand.

Tha mi caillte.

I am lost.

Mo ghràdh ort, chan fhaic mi tuilleadh gu brath thu.

My love, I'll never see you again.

ràn na mara

cry of the sea

hù a hó seo Bliadhn' Ùr

this New Year's Day

Ciamar a thilleas dòchas

How can hope return?

ACKNOWLEDGEMENTS

Thank you does not seem sufficient to acknowledge the continued warm and encouraging support for this work surrounding the IOLAIRE Disaster on both sides of the Atlantic—from Dr. Finley McLeod's telling me of the sinking on my first trip to the Isle of Lewis, to Rod Read's gift of the cover photo of The Beasts of Holm, to Turnstone's production of this beautiful book.

Malcolm MacDonald has been a mainstay, sharing historical knowledge, reams of his own research and responding to my endless questions. Mary Ferguson's initial help in the library continued through her multiple readings of the text, where she applied her patient and keen eye for detail to both the Gaelic and authenticity of place. Kathleen Milne arranged for the first public readings that drew encouraging response from the writer's group at the Stornoway Library. John MacLeod spontaneously sent galley proofs of *When I Heard the Bell*, the book invaluable in informing the voices in *Iolaire*. Appreciation is due, as well, to the Tolsta Historical Society, the *Stornoway Gazette* (Archives), the Stornoway Historical Society, John MacQueen, members of the World Navy Ships Forum, and many others.

The late Robert Kroetsch, writer and friend, noted the resonance between the IOLAIRE Disaster and the incomprehensible tragedies of our own time. His response affirmed the importance of telling this story. Deepest gratitude is owed to Dennis Cooley—master poet, mentor, editor, and friend—for inspiration, sustained interest, ever-gentle ministrations to the text, and sheer staying power. Thanks to St. John's College and St. Paul's College, University of Manitoba, colleagues, friends and family, and especially Vic.

I would also like to thank the following:

Aberdeen Journal
Am Baile Highland History and Culture
Archives and Special Collections, University of Manitoba
Fran Beckett
Francis Carroll
Sharon Caseburg
Peter Cunningham
Daily News [London]
Anne Dunlop
C. John Edwards
Sarah Ens
Evening Telegram [Angus]
Gazette and West Coast Advertiser
Glasgow Herald
Hebrides News
HM General Register House
Hull Daily Mail
Peter May, *The Lewis Trilogy*
Lloyd's Registry of Yachts
Marion (Mór) MacLeod
Meteorological Office Scotland
Roddy Murray
National Archives of Scotland
National Archives UK [Public Record Office]
National Library of Scotland
Navy List
North Tolsta Historical Society
Jamis Paulson
Agnes Rennie
St. Paul's College Library
St. Paul's College fellowship
School for Scottish Studies Archive, University of Edinburgh
Scotland On Sunday
The Scotsman
Scotsman on Sunday
Sea Sorrow: The Story of the Iolaire Disaster
Moti Shojania
siol-nan-gaidheal.org
Ian Crichton Smith
Ann Stinner
The Times [London]
Tolsta District News
The Tolsta Townships
University of Manitoba Libraries
Virtual Hebrides
Wendy MacDonald
Western Isles Library Stornoway
Kathryn Young